Skateboarding and the Senses

This book presents a new perspective on skateboarding, centered on the senses, skill acquisition, embodiment, and the concept of "city craft."

Skateboarding and the Senses traces how skaters use their skilled bodies to bring vitality to contested spaces. Building on sensory anthropology, the book draws connections between the diverse ways skaters move and their boundless drive for social action – from rebellious interventionism to a critical engagement with sportification and the Olympics. Coalescing around skateboarding's pedagogy of enskilment, the book examines what to make of the skater's way of sensing the city, of their bruised heels and scabbed elbows, and of their sensory attunement to their friends and foes. Grounded in historical, anthropological, and phenomenological theories of body and space, it examines how skaters acquire somatic knowledge and socio-emotional resilience through their sonic and vibratory experience of the city streets. This sensory anthropology of skateboarding reveals new insights into its long arc of subculture, lifestyle, and sport.

This is essential reading for anybody with an interest in the sociology, culture or history of sport, urban geographies, sensory studies, or social and cultural anthropology.

Sander Hölsgens is Assistant Professor in Anthropology at Leiden University, The Netherlands. He is a co-director of Pushing Boarders, a platform and international conference tracing the social impact of skateboarding worldwide. His popular writing on skateboarding has appeared in *Skateism*, *Vice*, and *Jenkem*. Together with Miriam Waltz and Mandy de Wilde, he currently runs the research project "Tracing pollution: practicing the anthropology of the more-than-human" (2023–2029).

Brian Glenney is Associate Professor in Philosophy at Norwich University in Vermont, USA. He works in both the fields of philosophy of perception and spatial justice. He is the co-editor of two volumes in Routledge's Rewriting the History of Philosophy Book Series: *Molyneux's Question and the History of Philosophy* and *The Senses and the History of Philosophy* and has written several peer-reviewed articles on spatial justice and skateboarding.

Routledge Focus on Sport, Culture and Society

Routledge Focus on Sport, Culture and Society showcases the latest cutting-edge research in the sociology of sport and exercise. Concise in form (20,000-50,000 words) and published quickly (within three months), the books in this series represents an important channel through which authors can disseminate their research swiftly and make an impact on current debates. We welcome submissions on any topic within the socio-cultural study of sport and exercise, including but not limited to subjects such as gender, race, sexuality, disability, politics, the media, social theory, Olympic Studies, and the ethics and philosophy of sport. The series aims to be theoretically-informed, empirically-grounded and international in reach, and will include a diversity of methodological approaches.

Available in this series:

Sport, Forced Migration and the 'Refugee Crisis'
Enrico Michelini

Sport Policy Across the United Kingdom
A Comparative Analysis
Edited by Mathew Dowling, Spencer Harris and Chris Mackintosh

Olympic Laws
Culture, Values, Tensions
Mark James and Guy Osborn

Sport and Social Media in Business and Society
Gashaw Abeza and Ryan King-White

Skateboarding and the Senses
Skills, Surfaces, and Spaces
Sander Hölsgens and Brian Glenney

For more information about this series, please visit: https://www.routledge.com/Routledge-Focus-on-Sport-Culture-and-Society/book-series/RFSCS

Skateboarding and the Senses
Skills, Surfaces, and Spaces

Sander Hölsgens and Brian Glenney

LONDON AND NEW YORK

First published 2025
by Routledge
4 Park Square, Milton Park, Abingdon, Oxon OX14 4RN

and by Routledge
605 Third Avenue, New York, NY 10158

Routledge is an imprint of the Taylor & Francis Group, an informa business

© 2025 Sander Hölsgens and Brian Glenney

The right of Sander Hölsgens and Brian Glenney to be identified as authors of this work has been asserted in accordance with sections 77 and 78 of the Copyright, Designs and Patents Act 1988.

The Open Access version of this book, available at www.taylorfrancis.com, has been made available under a Creative Commons Attribution-Non Commercial-No Derivatives (CC-BY-NC-ND) 4.0 license.

Any third party material in this book is not included in the OA Creative Commons license, unless indicated otherwise in a credit line to the material. Please direct any permissions enquiries to the original rightsholder.

Trademark notice: Product or corporate names may be trademarks or registered trademarks, and are used only for identification and explanation without intent to infringe.

British Library Cataloguing-in-Publication Data
A catalogue record for this book is available from the British Library

Library of Congress Cataloging-in-Publication Data
Names: Hölsgens, Sander, author. | Glenney, Brian, author.
Title: Skateboarding and the senses : skills, surfaces, and spaces / Sander Hölsgens and Brian Glenney. Description: New York : Routledge, 2025. | Series: Routledge focus on sport, culture and society | Includes bibliographical references and index.
Identifiers: LCCN 2024025867 | Subjects: LCSH: Skateboarding--Social aspects. | Streetscapes (Urban design) | Movement, Aesthetics of. | Senses and sensation. | Intuition. | Resilience (Personality trait) | Ethnology.
Classification: LCC GV859.8 H6525 2025 | DDC 306.4/83--dc23/eng/20240711
LC record available at https://lccn.loc.gov/2024025867

ISBN: 978-1-032-83972-1 (hbk)
ISBN: 978-1-032-83979-0 (pbk)
ISBN: 978-1-003-51064-2 (ebk)

DOI: 10.4324/9781003510642

Typeset in Times New Roman
by KnowledgeWorks Global Ltd.

Contents

Acknowledgments   *vi*

1 A Magical Bind: Writing Skate Culture   1

2 The Skater's Body: A Sensory Anthropology of Sideways Movement   13

3 Crafting the City: Embodied, Symbolic, and Engaged Skateboarding   29

4 Failure and the Senses: A Skate Pedagogy of Care and Resilience   46

5 Grey Pleasure: Skateboarding as a Deviant and Salubrious Ecology   60

6 Epilogue: Toward a Multispecies Futurity for Skateboarding   77

Index   *81*

Acknowledgments

Skateboarding, like writing, can be a magical experience. Writing about skateboarding is perhaps the most joyful research practice imaginable. The growing community of skate academics performs an ethos of care, kindness, and generosity remarkably close to the horizontality and collegiality in skateboarding. This truly is a community unlike any other. Thank you for crafting an academy that is effecting positive social change by being welcoming, fun, rigorous, and big-hearted.

Our gratitude goes to the following people for their knowledge, candor, and support in making this book possible: Dani Abulhawa, Ted Barrow, Igor Boog, Thomas Callan-Riley, Loïs Dejalle, Clifton Evers, Jacob Folsom-Fraster, Sophie Friedel, Stuart Maclure, Harry Meadley, Paul O'Connor, Ilse Prins, Camiel Roex, Sven Schaepkens, Jasper Verstappen, Neftalie Williams, and Indigo Willing.

Special thanks to the readers of our book for their astute remarks: Kyle Beachy, Patrick Kigongo, Judith Leijdekkers, Duncan McDuie-Ra, Paul O'Connor, Jasmijn Rana, and Francisco Vivoni. To our photographers, whose images make our arguments come to life: Taylor Ballard, Norma Ibarra, Louisa Menke, and Sarah Meurle. To Simon Whitmore and Rebecca Connor at Routledge, who made this a pleasant and exciting experience in academic publishing.

This book is generously supported by the Startersbeurs project "Tracing pollution through multimodal methods: practicing the anthropology of the more-than-human," generously offered by the Institute of Cultural Anthropology and Development Sociology at Leiden University.

1 A Magical Bind
Writing Skate Culture

The text before you is built on the premise that skateboarding is something magical. It's a sweaty, performative, ritualistic, and fetishized bind between a person and their built environment – interfaced by a wooden deck, two pivoting trucks, four polyurethane wheels, greasy bearings, and some nuts and bolts. Modern architecture is the skater's temple for trick play. Part of its allure is a resistance to being a sport or lifestyle or subculture or punk activity. What exactly skateboarding *is* or *represents* has been unclear since its origins in 1950s and 1960s in California and Japan's coastal regions.

Invigorated by the anthropology of the senses, we – two skaters-turned-researchers – believe that something as enchanting as skateboarding is best understood by attending to people's somatic behavior. In this book, we draw connections between the diverse ways skaters move and their historical drive for political action. The aim of the book is to grasp the skater's sensory world, conditioned by its relational and contingent urban ecologies (Rawes 2013). Skaters depend on and find joy in the kinds of materialities increasingly associated with the annihilation of human and nonhuman life: asphalt, iron, granite, steel. Urban space and its street furniture are a necessary ingredient for skate culture: the built environment affords the weird and beautiful trick play cardinal to street skating (O'Connor et al. 2023). Stronger yet, pollution – materialized in the modern city – makes urban leisure activities like skateboarding conceivable, if not pleasurable (Glenney 2023). Without the city, there is no skate culture. Without grey spaces, there is no enskiled creativity. Its practice is decidedly modern and therefore complicit to ecological damage. Skateboarding, to paraphrase Clifton Evers (2019), is polluted leisure. But it is also a *sensitive* form of leisure, as the socio-ecological precarity of the world is engaged in a decidedly multisensorial way (Zajchowski and Rose 2020). The skater's body, then, is a contaminated body. A sensory anthropology of skateboarding is needed to fully comprehend its repercussions: *what to make of the enskilment of trick play in the context of a damaged, dying planet?*

As we write this introduction, eco-conscious and ecosophic movements by and for skaters are emerging across the globe: whereas many a skater used to be entranced by the decades-old assertion to "skate and destroy," a growing number

DOI: 10.4324/9781003510642-1
This chapter has been made available under a CC-BY-NC-ND 4.0 license.

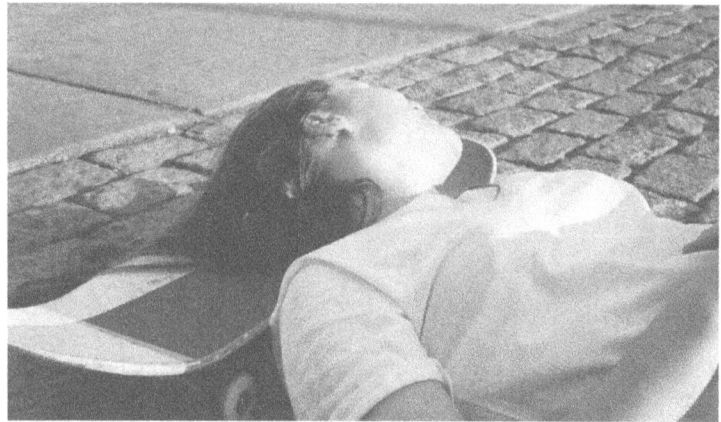

Figure 1.1 Skater Josie relaxing after a long skate session in Malmö, Sweden.
Source: Photo by Sarah Meurle.

of collectives turn to skateboarding for reparative ends. They ask, can we cook up a practice that is somewhat less reliant on destructive practices so as to speculate how skateboarding can become more earthly, caring, kind, and sustainable? This book foregrounds skateboarding as a sensory practice in order to deepen our understanding of the complex socio-historical relationship between the modern city and its diverse users. Our account of skateboarding is structured around the concept of enskilment – a set of bodily techniques and dispositions acquired not through formal education but via peer-based apprenticeship and self-regulated wayfinding. We trace why skaters fall and tumble, film and photograph, sweep sidewalks, wax ledges, and move sideways. Along the way, we might learn how the city casts the sensory spell that is skateboarding – its grit, scuffs, stench, filth, pollution, and sweat *and also* cleanliness, purity, order, and health.

Writing, skateboarding

The most thrilling prose on skateboarding is also a poetics of the built environment. Few people manage to do so eloquently or, should we say, authentically. Ted Barrow is known for his *Thrasher* series "This Old Ledge" and his Instagram persona *Feedback TS*. Anyone with a slight acquaintance will attest to his care for the written word. He has the capacity to convince malevolent administrators to look at skaters, to really look, and see what beauty they are up to. In the zine *Urban Pamphleteer #8 Skateboardings*, Barrow (2020: 2) writes,

> Find a curb, skate a curb. I've been skating this curb near my parent's house for nearly seven years. I still say 'my parent's house' even though

my father has been dead for nearly six years, just as my mother still hasn't changed the outgoing message on our answering machine. It's not that we are in denial – the void left by my father in my mother's house has an almost physical presence – it's just that home is both a place, and increasingly, a time. You know what I mean? Coming home from the holidays is like stepping back in time. As is, for me, a good curb ….

Accompanying his text is a square image. It is a black-and-white photograph, undeniably made by a tall person pointing a camera downward, toward the tarmac in front of them. Half of the image showcases bland asphalt, the other a suburban pavement: greyish, large tiles, emptied of greens. Separating asphalt and pavement is an archetypal curb: about four inches high in stature, fairly wide, and rough around the edges.

It's an unremarkable photograph. And yet. And yet we can imagine Ted Barrow skating there, in front of his parent's house, falling and tumbling and landing some tricks. To him, it's just a curb and it's just about everything. It's this curb in a plebeian suburban that gives a material form to his memories – joyful and otherwise. Like life, it's grainy and patchy. You can grease it with wax to smoothen its surface, but its underlying cracks will remain. This curb, *his* curb, is a testament to so much more than seven years of skating, to hours and hours of reappropriating mundane architectural space for extraordinary creativity. Here, a sociality, a *lifeworld*, is made visible through the granular materiality of stock pavement: this is any skater's history as much as it is Barrow's – "a temporal ownership you feel as you repurpose underutilized public space" (Vadi 2024: 60).

In some ways, Ted Barrow's text and image are a primordial example of ethnographic writing, of finding words to attend to the biographical, material, emotional, political, and ideological dimensions of a place. Barrow chooses to share the allure of a formulaic feature of the built environment – some granite creating an elevation on roadsides – and notices its binaries: life and death, forgetting and remembering, and landing a trick and failing miserably. It is a curb like any other, including those we as authors skate. It sparks the question: what about the crusts and cracks elsewhere, spaces that we make and care for, imagine, and remember. What about the driveways or streets or muddy roads in front of our family homes? *Find a curb, skate a curb*: it's an invitation to sense the city we live in.

Despite this text – and many others like it – Ted Barrow worries that his writing is not enough. At the skate conference *Pushing Boarders* (2018), he says:

> I moved to New York in 2002, wanting to be a skateboard writer and realised it's fucking hard. On the one hand, you're writing to a group of people who don't necessarily want to be written about. And otherwise you're explaining an activity to someone who's never stepped on a skateboard before. And that's imposing challenges for a writer.

The audience awes in recognition and anguish. It's 2 June 2018. The shallow London sun lights up a large conference room at The Bartlett School of Architecture, University College London. Across the room we notice hundreds of skateboards and about as many people. These are scholars, critics, journalists, nonprofit professionals, and blokes who simply love skating. It's the conference's second panel. Barrow's the moderator.

Earlier that morning, first-gen skate scholars Becky Beal, Iain Borden, and Ocean Howell discuss what it was like to be part of the first generation of academics to give serious attention to something as juvenile and futile as skateboarding. Somehow they managed to convince academic publishers and universities as early as the 1990s that it's worth zooming in on this quirky urban activity. Borden, a first-wave British skater and professor of urban culture, and professional skater/urban historian Howell speak to their excitement of writing about a community they're heavily invested in. They just had to find the words and theories to articulate the kinds of critical thoughts and feelings they've had for years: Borden (2001) pushed the idea of skateboarding as a poetics; Howell (2001) traces its enmeshment with hostile architecture and security. Beal's experience was rather different. Early on in her research projects, in the early 1990s, she had the opportunity to start skating herself but decided otherwise. This enabled Beal (1996) to study themes like gender relations and alternative masculinities from the position of an outsider: "I think insiders' perspectives are super important, but being an outsider, you can ask the naive questions that an insider can't ask" (Riordan 2022, online).

Ted Barrow holds a radically different position within this community. His rise to fame started with an impromptu Instagram account – *Feedback TS*. Starting alongside his graduate studies in art history, he invited skaters across the globe to submit skate videos. Like an art critic reeking in irony and sarcasm, he would bludgeon each video's performance. Barrow's critiques rode the hobby horse of skating's most beloved topics: skinny jeans and baggy trousers, the size and shape of boards, the beauty of ridiculed tricks, and the architectural history of skate spots. For a good couple of years, *Feedback TS* inhabited a unique slot in a culture that otherwise resisted most verbal and written forms of critique, commentary, and analysis. Barrow knows how "fucking hard" it is to be a skate writer: it's this phrase he uses to kickstart the panel discussion, aptly called "What We Do is Secret: The Challenge of Writing about Skateboarding" (Pushing Boarders 2018).

All panelists know that to utter a word about skateboarding, instead of simply doing it, is to begin in failure and admit defeat. Skateboarding is tacit, performed, and thus rarely understood discursively, if ever. We know the only response to Barrow's truth is to go outside again and skate, or to speak in clichés. The best we can do at a panel is not talk about the sensation of skating itself but discuss all things proximate. One discussant shares a horrid experience when they had to protect themselves by using a skateboard as a shield. Another, how there is no such thing as independent skate journalism:

corporate money decides what's being published and censored. Yet another, why skateboarding is full of rituals, spiritual depth, and even religious tendencies. We discuss all things seemingly adjacent to skateboarding, yet decidedly close to the sensory ecology of skateboarding. The feeling of riding a skateboard is located achingly close to the angst of being harassed by a security guard. The pleasure of grinding on a curb reaffirms the sacrality of architecture. And the snapping sound of slams and bails is interwoven with the sonic knowledge skaters hold of both their body and their surroundings. *What skaters do may be best kept like a secret, held by the senses.* Yet this somatic secret is the exact topic of the chapters to come.

University of skate

We – Brian and Sander – first met during Pushing Boarders London, in 2018. Sander co-organized the conference, while Brian was an invited discussant during its inaugural Academic Forum. At the time, Sander had just finished his ethnography on Seoul's skate scene, while Brian was tailoring his interest in the philosophy of perception to skateboarding as an embodied praxis. As much as Pushing Boarders consolidated an academic community of skate scholars, our paths only crossed tangentially: we collaborated with the same people, though never together; we both focused on enskilment and the senses, howbeit from different disciplinary backgrounds; we engaged in skate activism despite being based in different pockets of the world; and perhaps most formatively, we both affirmed, in our publications, that skateboarding was a mystery, an enigma that resists definition. This book speaks to our lifelong pursuit of critically engaging the skateboarding world we are a part of: we stand on the shoulders of scholars who draw upon their own positionality as skaters and show us the importance of participatory approaches and grassroots methodologies within academia (Abulhawa 2020; McDuie-Ra 2023; Willing and Pappalardo 2023).

Bridging the acts of moving sideways and writing seated resulted in a continuous flow of action research. We actively crafted and constructed our theoretical reflections and case studies in close proximity to skateboarding's ever-changing ecology. While not an ethnography in the traditional sense of the word, our book builds upon a decidedly praxis-based endeavor: alongside academic publications and critical analyses of skate media, we add a broader arrangement of research materials—skateboards, city streets, skate shops, sneakers, do-it-yourself (DIY) builds, nuts and bolts, wax, and, of course, other skaters. What's more, our bodies are a meaningful site of knowing and sensing the world, as much as they are a relational interface: a built rapport with skaters through our shared praxis and collective exploration of how one's body "involves itself with and orients itself towards the world" (Chamarette 2012: 37). As such, we draw upon our long-term involvement in and research on situated scenes in South Korea, the Netherlands, and US' coastal regions –

thematically structured around issues of activism, embodiment, sportification, and prefiguration.

Duncan McDuie-Ra (2023) conceptualizes such an approach as a "rolling ethnography," considering skateboarding as a valid mode of research, alongside social scientific methods like walking, observing, listening, surveying, and interviewing. This enskiled and corporeal sensibility resonates with feminist methodologies in action sports, which aim to instill an engaged and reflexive approach in social research (Willing and Pappalardo 2023). And yet, despite our embedded positionality, we actively refuse to claim an insider's perspective in order to legitimize our writing or argumentation. As much as we are speaking to our experiences as skaters, the epistemological binaries of "anthropologist/informant, expert/object, and knower/known" (Weis 2016, online) tend to engender problematic forms of objectification, control, and hierarchy. Our experiences as skaters orbit our writing style, topical interest, and referential framework, instead of being a prerogative of our role as researchers. Rather than claiming ownership of this cultural domain of leisure, we consider our identity marker as skaters as but one formative element of our positionality.

We resist a totalizing universality of a skater's identity, challenging the illusion of separation between skaters and fellow members of the public. Instead, we believe that a pointed inquiry into skateboarding as a sensory ecology holds meaning and significance for analogous studies into the body, perception, and enskilment. The ontological statements we make in this book serve to draw connections between the particularity of skate culture – performed differently across the globe – and related practices of sports, leisure, and craft. Rather than writing about skateboarding as an integral whole, we are interested in the process of sense-making through relational and positional writing. This speaks to the current state of skate scholarship, which seeks to expand its disciplinary focus from subcultural studies and lifestyle sports to fields as diverse as phenomenology, critical race theory, performance, indigenous studies, anthropology, medicine, law, and philosophy. As Paul O'Connor (2024: 1) argues, only now can we identify "a nascent movement in skateboard studies to craft and adopt bespoke methodologies that speak to the specificities of skateboarding as a social, sensual and urban act." The aim of this book is to push skateboarding's discourse on the senses and experiential, the somatic and affective.

Writing this book felt like a good skate session with friends: it was organized chaos. In a session, skaters share the space of a skatepark or street, turning their bodily praxis toward their peers. Occasionally, skaters decide to collectively focus on a specific obstacle, taking turns and observing each other's attempts, not one-upping but playing off each other's emplaced proceedings. Existing somewhere between comradery and self-improvement, such a session is both individual and collaborative, playful and scholastic, painful and pleasurable. Performing tricks alongside one another can inspire, generate a sense of competition, or trigger other emotive responses: it's a way to embolden one's own techniques, enjoy the bodily performativity of peers, and cultivate creativity by association. Akin to improv theater, skate sessions have a narrative arc based on happenstance and creativity, mutually transforming everyone and everything around them.

Similar to how aging skaters start a session by rolling warm-ups, i.e. trying not to fall, our writing process began by loosening up our research – sharing snippets of thoughts, scribbling autoethnographic vignettes, experimenting with theoretical considerations, and jumping on early-morning video calls. The point of these exercises was prefigurative, never to design a structure for a book-length project, or a long-form text as such. Instead, these preliminary methods helped us feel and articulate how our researching bodies are oriented by and toward skateboarding. Sara Ahmed (2006: 236) writes how orientations "are about how we begin, how we proceed from 'here' (…) as the zero-point of orientation, the point from which the world unfolds." By decentering the aim of publishing a paper or book, the academic equivalent to landing a banger trick, we carved out a space for experimentation and perspectival variation. Put differently, we sessioned. Skateboarding, including writing about skateboarding, cannot originate in a pre-planned seriousness but reveals itself in play that occasionally finds a sustainable line of thought. To attune to and queer our relationality to skateboarding presupposes that we held one another culpable for our epistemological impulses. Skate-writing this line together mimics the reciprocity between a skater (actor) and their filmer (observer), both of whom regularly switch roles as they collaboratively work toward trick play and its documentation.

Relatedly, we are aware of the potential repercussions of publishing our research on skate culture, not least because it is increasingly coopted by municipalities and sports associations to shape their policies. Our writing may adversely or positively affect the lifeworlds of our skating friends. Deborah D'Amico-Samuels (2010: 74) writes that many anthropologists are "protected from the emotional implications and political responsibilities they might otherwise feel as a result of their experiences during anthropological research." As our rapport with the skate community exceeds the framework of a research project, the impact of our work is immediately palpable: the methods we use do not operate as a "distancing device" (idem: 75). We share spaces with the people whose lifeworlds we describe and work we cite, both in public and private settings, signifying that our writing is politically and emotionally accountable to the communities we're connected to.

This mutual interplay between academic discourse and skate culture gives shape to this book in yet another way. While the scholarly interest in skateboarding is rapidly growing, the community of skate researchers remains tight-knit – translating the prefigurative horizontality of its ethos into an academic context. Contemporary skate studies is punctuated by a collegial fabric, where more established scholars actively engage in uplifting researchers in precarity to foster cooperative care. More practically, we've skated alongside many of the skate scholars we reference, being not only theoretically or intellectually connected to their work but also sensorially attuned to their sideways movements. Our citational practice coincides with the intentional process of community formation in skate studies, fostering ongoing practices of relation and belonging inspired by conscientious movements like #CiteBlackWomen and #SayHerName (Shange 2022). Building a relational web of critical writing on skateboarding, we consider how citation can generate recognition in wider academic contexts – advancing a skate ethos of solidarity, generosity, and care.

Finally, a comment about the length of this book. For art historian Carol Mavor (2012: 15), books on pleasure "are always in danger of not getting the affect right *and* of self-indulgence. Better to keep it thin." We would like to add: what makes a skate session pleasurable is that not all tricks are attempted, let alone landed. Some are attempted, others only imagined, locating a performance of the full sensory register of skate invariably beyond reach. The brevity of this book reverberates the flow of a session: we rigorously center our attention to a finite set of topical issues, which we approach from various disciplinary angles, to arrive at a provisional set of conclusions, to which we will return to again for more play. Reading this book takes most readers about as long as a singular skate session of a full afternoon or the timeframe of a couple lunch breaks. Its cadence is one of short theorizations, exploratory lines of argumentation, spellbinding examples, and edged conclusions. Our language, mimicking skate tricks, is necessarily pulsating with urgency but never fully exhaustive.

Figure 1.2 Fabiana Delfino tweaks a hurricane in Los Angeles.
Source: Photo by Taylor Ballard.

Skateboarding and the senses

Beginning as a DIY activity by youth in the 1950s and 1960s, and coopted by surf culture in the 1970s, skateboarding became a decidedly urban activity in the 1980s (Borden 2001). It has since produced multi-millionaires like Yuto Horigome, Nyjah Huston, and Leticia Bufoni; mainstream conglomerates like *Supreme*, *Polar*, and *Vans*; and an athletic sport since its inclusion in the Olympic Games. Yet, remarkably, skateboarding sustains much of its transgressive and countercultural identity, making for some difficulty in finding a comprehensive definition. Skateboarding is positional rather than institutional, taking definitional structures and overwriting them with their opposite (Geckle and Shaw 2022). In doing so, skateboarding resists some of its classification and thereby resists control, a *definiens* that fits the *definiendum* (Lundry 2003).

This book argues that an inquiry into embodiment may generate meaningful insights into skateboarding as a multifaceted cultural expression, without the need for reductionist classification. Our aim is fourfold: first, to articulate the primacy and immediacy of a sensorium of skate, structured around tacit, emplaced, and stanced ways of knowing. Second, to center the senses as the basis of a horizontal pedagogy in skateboarding, by tracing how it feels to become enworlded as a skater in relation to others (Romero 2020). Third, to foreground how skateboarding is experienced differently across time and space, countering the oft-made argument that skaters are a homogeneous culture sharing a universal habitus. And fourth, to trace how skate culture is enveloped in social-ecological realities of urban hostility and environmental pollution.

The history of the senses in anthropology intimates the generative potential of sensuous scholarship within the context of technique-driven praxes like skateboarding. From Marcel Mauss' (1973) early theory on the intersection of bodily techniques and morality to Cristina Grasseni's (2022) skilled visions, and from Steven Feld's (2021) sensuous epistemologies to Elena Guzman and Emily Hong's (2022) feminist sensory ethnography, the body has been an existential ground for studying socialities and cultures for many a decade. The sensory turn, kickstarted in the early 1990s by scholars including David Howes, Paul Stoller, and Constance Classen, has been especially important in showcasing that the senses are socially modeled rather than being innate tendencies of humanity as such or immutable patterns of specific cultures.

The aim of sensuous scholarship is not to classify but rather to accept sensuousness and "lend one's body to the world and accept its complexities, tastes, structures, and smells" (Stoller 1997: xvii–xviii). As the senses are relationally produced, socially cultivated, and culturally attuned, a sensory investigation into skateboarding accounts for the entanglements between bodies, socialities, and environs. Following Anna Harris (2020), we take as a starting point that "sensing is not something innate (i.e., you are born with it), cognitive/neurological (in the brain) or individual but rather *cultivated through social, bodily, material practices.*" Sensing is an epistemology, a knowledge system acquired through socio-historical, environmental, and political entanglements – all of which reverberate through and coincide with the specific sensibilities of a given body. Bodily perception, then, is mediated by the body *in situ*: our case studies enable us to elicit the sensory worlds skaters make and use to experience, navigate, and interpret their clime.

An anthropological inquiry into the senses also draws attention to how experiences operate across axes of gender, ethnicity, class, sexuality, and ability – located at "intersectional coming-togethers of space, time, and material made manifest through the sensing of bodily movement" (Carter et al. 2022: 242). Simultaneously, it offers a critique of the idea that tools or environs have intrinsic affordances. A skateboard and the built environment are co-produced by social values and cultural norms. In particular, we theorize this production of space and the tuning of sensorial models of knowing by positioning skateboarding in close proximity to an epistemic culture of making. More specifically, we conceptualize skateboarding as a craft of the city. This understanding is especially pressing with the emergence of skateboarding being made into a sport, an institutional attempt being its Olympic inclusion, pivoting its pedagogy from enskilment and horizontal apprenticeship to a serious athleticism with top-down coached training regimens.

Learning to skate in the built environment echoes practices like mushroom hunting in forests, described by anthropologist Anna Tsing (2015) as an art of noticing. Learning to notice something, to discriminate between useless and useful phenomena, is a decidedly embodied practice. It implies cultivating a bodily register to attend to what's meaningful: from matsutake mushrooms in the forest undergrowth to skateable spots among urban detritus. Like mushroom hunting, skateboarding is learned by doing – by training the body to sense, discern, and be attentive. Such a sensory education, we attest alongside Tsing, is enveloped in contingent ecological and capitalist systems – denoting much more than the bare techniques themselves. Skaters are intimately familiar with the ruins of the Anthropocene, creatively reappropriating its grey spaces for trick play and, at times, activism. They do so in a situated way, attending to local communities, site-specific spatialities, and divergent sensory models of experience. Perhaps this is best described as plural and variegated, referring to "the diverse spectrum of *skateboardings*, and the hundred visions and revisions of what skateboarding is to each skateboarder" (Callan-Riley and Hölsgens 2020: i).

Throughout this book, we invoke the anthropology of the senses by attending to how skaters learn to make sense of the built environment (Hölsgens 2024). While the brevity of this book means we must be selective in our literature review, we will invoke the sensibilities and epistemological considerations of such sensuous scholarship in the chapters to come. In Chapter 2, we articulate how skateboarding proposes a multifaceted sensorium. What a skater sees, hears, feels, smells, and kinesthetically perceives is a study in contrast: a feast of the sweet adrenaline of success and a bitter quinine of injury, the hostile sensation of risk, and the anticipatory feeling of landing a trick. This chapter theorizes the sensory density of skateboarding, zooming in on its sensorium, and zooming out to capture its social history of *in situ* change. In Chapter 3, we start by considering skateboarding as an epistemic culture. Building upon the discourse of craft, we argue that skaters engage in a plurality of complementary learning strategies. It is, we argue, a city craft – situated in grey urban space and structured around an entanglement of emplaced knowing, horizontal apprenticeship, and antirank ethos.

The second half of the book points toward the variegated sensory dimensions of skateboarding (Carter et al. 2022). Chapter 4 shows how skateboarding is punctuated by a history of failure. Analyzing how the "Skate and Destroy" mantras are represented in skate videos, we scrutinize its hegemonic representations of failure – echoing neoliberal ideas of self-reliance and achievement. This chapter then introduces Skate Like a Girl, a nonprofit organization that queers such narratives by proposing communal and reparative experiences of failure. Chapter 5 seeks to understand the entanglements between skateboarding and the modern city. Rethinking skateboarding as a polluted form of pleasure, we explore how skaters engage the hostility of the built environment – ranging from deviant illegality to performative activism. Our final chapter looks at skate-friendly ecologies, bringing together concrete jungles and wild spaces. Here, we argue that skateboarding offers the possibility to sense the city anew, not least by engaging in restorative practices of care.

References

Abulhawa, D. (2020). *Skateboarding and Femininity: Gender, Space-Making and Expressive Movement*. London: Routledge.

Ahmed, S. (2006). *Queer Phenomenology: Orientations, Objects, Others*. Durham: Duke University Press.

Barrow, T. (2020). "Find a Curb." In Hölsgens, S. & Callan-Riley, T. (eds.). *Urban Pamphleteer #8 Skateboardings*, 1–2. London: UCL Urban Laboratory.

Beal, B. (1996). "Alternative Masculinity and Its Effects on Gender Relations in the Subculture of Skateboarding." *Journal of Sport Behavior*, 19.3: 204–220.

Borden, I. (2001). *Skateboarding, Space and the City: Architecture and the Body*. Oxford: Berg Publishers.

Callan-Riley, T., & Hölsgens, S. (2020). *Urban Pamphleteer# 8 Skateboardings*. London: Urban Laboratory.

Carter, T. F., Heath, S., Jacobs, S., & Rana, J. (2022). "Sensory Ecologies: the Refinement of Movement and the Senses in Sport." *The Senses and Society*, 17.3: 241–251.

Chamarette, J. (2012). *Phenomenology and the Future of Film*. Hampshire: Palgrave Macmillan.

D'Amico-Samuels, D. (2010). "Undoing Fieldwork: Personal, Political, Theoretical and Methodological Implications." In Harrison, F. (ed.). *Decolonizing Anthropology: Moving Further toward and Anthropology for Liberation. Third* Edition, 68–87. Arlington, Virginia: AAA.

Evers, C. (2019). "Polluted Leisure." *Leisure Sciences*, 41.5: 423–440.
Feld, S. (2021). "Places Sensed, Senses Placed: Toward a Sensuous Epistemology of Environments." In Howes, D. (ed.). *Empire of the Senses*, 179–191. London: Routledge.
Geckle, B., & Shaw, S. (2022). "Failure and Futurity: The Transformative Potential of Queer Skateboarding." *YOUNG*, 30.2: 132–148.
Glenney, B. (2023). "Polluted Leisure Enskilment: Skateboarding as Ecosophy." *Leisure Sciences*, 2023: 1–25.
Grasseni, C. (2022). "More than Visual: The Apprenticeship of Skilled Visions." *Ethos*, 2022: 1–19.
Guzman, E. H., & Hong, E. (2023). "Feminist Sensory Ethnography: Embodied Filmmaking as a Politic of Necessity." *Visual Anthropology Review*, 38.2: 184–210.
Harris, A. (2020). *A Sensory Education*. London: Routledge.
Hölsgens, S. (2024). "Learning to See Or How to Make Sense of the Skillful Things Skateboarders Do." In Vannini, P. (ed.). *The Routledge International Handbook of Sensory Ethnography*, 387–400. New York: Routledge.
Howell, O. (2001). "The Poetics of Security: Skateboarding, Urban Design, and the New Public Space." *Urban Action*, 2001: 64–86.
Lundry, W. (2003). "To Classify… Is to Control." *Thrasher Magazine*, 267: 134–139.
Mauss, M. (1973). "Techniques of the Body." *Economy and Society*, 2.1: 7–88.
Mavor, C. (2012). *Black and Blue*. Durham: Duke University Press.
McDuie-Ra, D. (2023). "Play Space in Plain Sight: The Disruptive Alliances between Street Trees and Skateboarders." *International Journal of Play*, 12.3: 285–303.
O'Connor, P. (2024). "Conceptualizing Grey Spaces in Skateboarding: Generating Theory and Method for Use beyond the Board." *International Review for the Sociology of Sport*, 2024 (online first): 1–18.
O'Connor, P., Evers, C., Glenney, B., & Willing, I. (2023). "Skateboarding in the Anthropocene: Grey Spaces of Polluted Leisure." *Leisure Studies* 42.6: 897–907.
Pushing Boarders (2018). *What we Do is Secret: The Challenge of Writing about Skateboarding*, https://www.youtube.com/watch?v=LaLbPMQulWQ.
Rawes, P. (2013). *Relational Architectural Ecologies: Architecture, Nature and Subjectivity*. London: Routledge.
Riordan, S. (2022). The OG skate scholar: an interview with Becky Beal. *Yeah Girl*, https://yeahgirlmedia.com/the-og-skate-scholar-an-interview-with-becky-beal/.
Romero, N. (2020). "You're Skating on Native Land: Queering and Decolonizing Skate Pedagogy." *Cultural and Pedagogical Inquiry*, 12.1: 230–243.
Shange, S. (2022). "Citation as Ceremony: #SayHerName, #CiteBlackWomen, and the Practice of Reparative Enunciation." *Cultural Anthropology*, 37.2: 191–198.
Stoller, P. (1997). *Sensuous Scholarship*. Philadelphia: University of Pennsylvania Press.
Tsing, A. T. (2015). *The Mushroom at the End of the World: On the Possibility of Life in Capitalist Ruins*. Princeton: Princeton University Press, https://press.princeton.edu/books/paperback/9780691220550/the-mushroom-at-the-end-of-the-world.
Vadi, J. (2024). *Chipped: Writing from a Skateboarder's Lens*. New York: Catapult.
Weis, M. (2016). "Collaboration". *Cultural Anthropology* online, https://culanth.org/fieldsights/series/collaboration.
Willing, I., & Pappalardo, A. (2023). *Skateboarding, Power and Change*. Berlin: Springer.
Zajchowski, C. A., & Rose, J. (2020). "Sensitive Leisure: Writing the Lived Experience of Air Pollution." *Leisure Sciences*, 42.1: 1–14.

2 The Skater's Body
A Sensory Anthropology of Sideways Movement

We don't know when stances were first discovered, much less when humans first discovered that their body could move sideways. Surfing, an activity that predates skateboarding by centuries, if not millennia, provides a provisional answer. Early surfers – documented in European historiographies across the 1700s and 1800s – did not stand sideways but laid on their belly or sat on their reed boats and wooden boards. For Polynesian natives, canoe surfing was a tool for transportation and coastal foraging, a leisure activity, and a spiritual practice (Hough-Snee and Eastman 2017). Those that stood were first recorded in the nineteenth century, and predominantly did so face-forward like a mono-skier (Moser 2008). Sideways surfing was incidentally documented: an engraved image accompanying a 1831 travelogue by missionary William Ellis chronicles an oceanic scene – usually considered the first Western illustration of surfing (Blakely 2014). The scene's protagonist uses a narrow plank to ride a tumble of waves, his left foot facing forward. And yet, it took until 1962 before anyone talked about "having a stance," with the first written record of a surfer being "goofy-footed" (Muirhead 1962). Remarkably, this was only five years after commercial skateboards were being produced (Borden 2001a), the moment skateboarding "broke out of the realm of casual play" (Davidson 1976: 14).

This timeline opens the possibility that skaters were the first to give words to being stanced. We can imagine a group of savvy sidewalk surfers bombing down a hill on their homemade boards on a waveless California day, in the late 1950s. The open space of the steep streets allows one of them to observe the others, pondering why her friends orient themselves with a different foot, leftways as opposed to her rightways stance. We see her whizzing by over the cement, as the grinding metal of her board's wheels makes a rattling, grating sound. She shouts at her friends: "you guys are so goofy!" The others look down at their feet and notice the footed difference. One of them retorts: "you are so regular!" – a real burn in America's cool culture of the 1950s. Later, they bring their stanced awareness to the water, and the rest is history.

Anachronistically, we can even imagine a prehistoric discovery of stance: did Peking man throw a spear goofy? After all, those who have discovered their stance find it as natural as handedness, making its socio-biological history as alluring as it is revolutionary. Perhaps, we speculate, stance fills a missing link in the story of human evolution, up there with opposable thumbs, upright movement, and tool usage. We might speculate further: the attentional resources, sensory abilities, and proto-social emotions cued by our ancestors awaken when a body finds its stance, adding potential evidence to the claim that skateboarding and surfing, as spot-hunting cultures, provide a significant advantage in navigating urban and oceanic spaces. But we digress.

This chapter articulates a sensorium of skateboarding: its sights and sounds, feelings and smells, kinesthesia and tactility, proprioception, and shifting sensations. How do they make sense of and give sense to the city? Is there such a thing as a skater's way of sensing? And in what ways are a skater's perceptive experience mediated by the social, spatial, and symbolic order of the built environment? An inquiry into sensuous abilities, we hold, offers a generative framework for tracing how skaters become emplaced and enworlded. Recognizing that such a sensorium is a figuration of a multiplicity of site-specific practices, this chapter offers a starting point for understanding how skateboarding is localized and individualized – mutually contingent on situated subject positions. We open this chapter with a brief literature review on skateboarding's ways of sensing, from its history of ocularcentrism to a recent appreciation of multisensoriality and somatics. We then turn to the peculiar ways in which skaters habitually use their senses to scout for and identify architectural space readily available for trick play. As such, we make the argument that skaters acquire bodily techniques in relation to their environs, attuning to the specific characteristics of the built environment and its sociality.

Moving sideways[1]

Why did humans learn to move sideways? Sensorially, it is not an intuitive movement: unlike crabs, we need to move our head and core to see where we're heading, pressuring our central nervous system along the way. From a socio-historical perspective, it holds both ludic and political meanings. The sideways *position* unlocks many ways for the human body to move, an entire axis of activity. This includes sports like baseball, golf, hockey, tennis, and pickleball. Militia and fighting strategies involve sideways *orientations*, as do archery and shoveling. Some of these practices, including javelin throwing and golf swinging, are *handed*. Practitioners use hand tools – a club, a spear, a bat – and usually think of themselves as right- or left-handed. By contrast, martial arts like Taekwondo and boxing are *footed*, structuring bodily techniques around a dominant leg. We are sure there are exceptions for how to distinguish handed from footed sports, but the point is: all these activities include sideways motilities dependent on a dominant limb.

Stance, by contrast, reconfigures the body itself as being laterally oriented, cultivating a plethora of sensorial, symbolic, and social meanings. As a below-the-knee-activity, you might imagine footedness as a central determining factor for skateboarding's sideways orientation. But preliminary studies suggest no correlation between a person's dominant foot or hand and their stance (Alexandre 2023). Whereas handedness and footedness are overwhelmingly "right dominant," the difference between a goofy and regular stance is near chance (Nootens and Harrison-Caldwell 2017). This begs the question: what is it about planks and boards that link them with a stanced orientation rather than its footedness?

Perhaps phenomenology offers a generative starting point. If anything, it's the dominant theoretical framework used to make sense of the skater's corporeality, their toes and fingers and twists and turns. It positions bodily experience as one of perceptual immediacy, seemingly unmatched for the study of wheeled sensorial orientations tailored to the perfection of tricks. Consider this example by phenomenologist Maurice Merleau-Ponty:

> For each object, as for each picture in an art gallery, there is an optimum distance from which it requires to be seen, a direction viewed from which it vouchsafes most of itself: at a shorter or greater distance we have merely a perception blurred through excess or deficiency. We therefore tend towards the maximum of visibility, and seek a better focus as with a microscope [...] The distance from me to the object is not a size which increases or decreases, but a tension which fluctuates round a norm.
> (1945[2013]: 352)

What is considered an optimum distance to look at pictures is not given but rather a technique embedded in a cultural context. Rather than an object readily available for research, like a scroll to be read, a body "is a living entity by which, and through which, we actively experience the world" (Desjarlais and Jason Throop 2011: 89). For phenomenologists, this living, existential body is a degree zero for our experience of and engagement with our environment. There is a particular interest in the entanglements between the immediacy of perception and broader socio-political forces.

What's more, to a phenomenologist, a bodily space is reshaped by the tools and equipment we use. The example most frequently used, and coopted from Martin Heidegger, is the hammer.

> Taken strictly, there 'is' no such thing as *an* equipment. To the being of any equipment there always belongs a totality of equipment, in which it can be this equipment that it is. Equipment is essentially 'something in-order-to.'
> (Heidegger 1927[1962]: 31).

A hammer, following this logic, is no tool with a flexible set of possible affordances. Rather, it is a piece of equipment – enveloped in the carpenter's toolkit – used *in-order-to* put to a specific kind of work, namely hammering.

Such a tool doesn't have to be observed or theorized before using. Instead, it simply takes on the role of the extension of our body, provided we are skilled hammer-users. Translating this phenomenological insight to the practice of skateboarding, one could argue that the skater's body becomes wheeled: the skateboard is a tool *in-order-to* glide. This use-case affects your possible actions and activities, including bolting eye-cry fast down hills and flying gut-drop high in the air (Loland and Bäckström 2023). For a phenomenologist, a skateboard as a tool inherently "affords" sideways actions, like gliding or riding. Following this line of logic, there are appropriate and less appropriate approaches for doing so.

Like tuning a guitar by turning the keys until hearing a harmonizing frequency, one can attune to the spatiality and temporality of a space or society through the movements of one's body to find its unique harmony until they are in lockstep, inseparable, and self-regulating – *clicked in*. This means becoming an interlocked whole: subject/object/environment. Rather than being a "mental script" or a taught model, enskilment is a set of bodily dispositions learned by doing. This involves situated and horizontal pedagogies, where the learner may mimic but is never formally taught by the expert. Instead, it is an education of attention, where the learner shapes their worldview through their engagement with a sociality of practitioners (cf. Gowlland 2019; Ingold 2000). This form of "enskilment" presents three intersecting parts for achieving this attunement, optimum context, or appropriate use-case of tools (cf. Pálsson 1994; Woods et al. 2021). One becomes enskiled in 1) a taskspace or an emplaced pattern of activity, by 2) a sensory attention to this pattern through the movement of one's body, which creates 3) a self-regulated, yet community-driven wayfinding that continuously matches the taskspace to bodily movement until interlocked. These three parts result in an "enskiled performer": an expert at a sensory craft.

Enskilment comes at you, fast, requiring intuitive bodily adjustments that are only slowed by reflection, quickened by reaction. Sensorially, this can be understood by the following: when skating, the aim is to "get things right," by identifying skateable space, performing successful tricks, or skating in a way that simply clicks. When the board has the appropriate weight, attire fits well, and the city's surface feels right, you just know it all belongs together, as does anyone observing you. Skaters, one could argue, seek this optimum fit by first acquiring and then maintaining this tacit know-how through enskilment. This optimum context is emplaced, meaning that the specific socio-spatial configurations of the built environment or other dominant cultural markers may affect the process of seeking bodily dispositions that feel right. Through enskilment, skaters find their place in the world, developing a capacity to use their body as a principal locus for filtering sensory input and discriminating what's meaningful (i.e., *skateable*) or not (Hölsgens 2018). As an epistemic culture, like other crafts like boat making or weaving, skaters work toward and maintain a situated know-how.

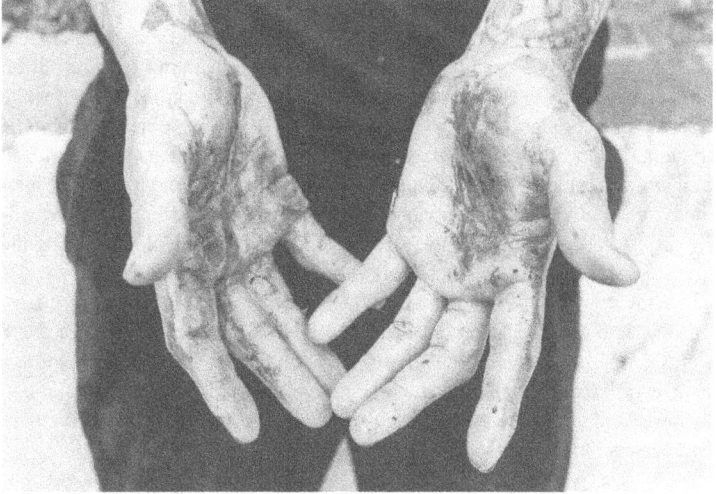

Figure 2.1 The bloodied hands of Johnny Tassopoulos after a heavy skate session.
Source: Photo by Taylor Ballard.

Subverting expectations

What if there is no optimal way to use a skateboard? What if skaters perform a critique of Merleau-Ponty's example of optimizing the angle to view a painting, or of Heidegger's deterministic understanding of the hammer as tool? What if the point of skateboarding is neither one of maximalism and success nor one of standardized somatics and normative trick play? Perhaps we need to attend to a more complex mode of emplaced subject formation – one which offers a radical alternative to the persistent schema of the skater's body (or the surfer, carpenter, and museum visitor) as a neuter. Given the importance of stance, a slight shift to this bodily schema may radically alter one's orientation, revealing a secret worldview unknown to those who continue their search for somatic perfectionism.

Take the example of switching one's stance. Professional skater Salman Agah is known for pushing the idea that skating switch is not only possible but also could be part of every skater's repertoire, essentially doubling the possibilities of tricks, symbolic meanings, and stylistic individuation. Confusing some onlookers, shifting between stance means appreciating, rather than resolving, impractical and ineffective motility. Skaters who learn to switch their stance have to come to terms with the, at times, adverse, unnatural, and dangerous feeling of such techniques. For what's front-facing becomes backward, what's left right, and what's intuitive artificial. In some ways, this is similar to writing or throwing a ball with your non-dominant hand. The main difference is that stance structures your full orientation: your outlook on the world is shifted, including your balance, proprioception, eyesight, and breakfall techniques. Using Merleau-Ponty's example, it's like looking at a painting using a mirror. Or, perhaps more apt, it's like painting using your non-dominant hand, while also looking through a mirror and standing on a moving object. With some training, it's most certainly doable, but it sensorially reorients your approach of a task-at-hand. Skating switch is a puzzling thing of beauty that never feels quite right, unlike the phenomenologist's desire to optimize their intuitive bodily disposition. It's pushing against the grain of normative play, uplifting the graceless and gawky – as if shouting in delight, "I have two left feet!"

While filming his video part for Emerica's *Stay Gold* (Miner 2010), Taiwanese-American skater Jerry Hsu endured severe leg injuries. These were followed by multiple ankle and knee surgeries. Rather than prioritizing his recovery, like many professional athletes would, Hsu decided to push through by switching his stance. As such, the video molds a public figure of creativity and perseverance. As Hsu says,

> Ok, so imagine your right knee had a really bad injury that you're recovering from. Whenever you ollie, you pop off your right foot. That's the foot that will propel you. Your other foot will lift you but it's that right foot that snaps off the ground and pushes you into the air. Well, my back knee was so hurt at the time that I couldn't skate normal, but I could skate switch. So, it was completely the injury. I did film a few things that were regular but they just weren't all that good. I think [filmmaker Jon] Miner made a good choice with the switch theme because it made the whole thing much stronger. […] He gave it a story to make up for my injuries.
> (Whiteley 2015, online).

Skating switch is not the opposite of Hsu's dominant mode of orientation but rather its aching lining. In Hsu's case, it is a way to circumvent an injury but not just: his switch stance communicates an affect and a politic, as much as it displays an awkward technique. Pushing back against a dominant stance is an enculturation: the point, here, is not to maximize the affordances of the plank or board but rather to break the rules by subverting the body's intuitive mode of engaging the world. Hsu shows that there is pleasure in reorienting oneself, in the face of an aching body. It is as if the knee injury unlocks a structure for unveiling somatic truths: how we move in the way we do, and why this matters. This, too, forces spectators to consider their expectations of the extreme athleticism skaters are known for. There's something decidedly unaesthetic about skating switch: the awkward push, the ungraceful shoulder movements, the apprehensive gaze.

But skateboarding has never been about hegemonic beauty or about the rule of thirds or divine-like bodies or formal principles. For long, it's been treated as a subculture because of its inimitable values and practices because of its rejection of the economic and political and aesthetic. Skating switch is a negation of the classicist notion of beauty as something eternal, symmetrical, uniform, and perfect. It orbits ideas of the weird and the ugly, seeking elegance in the irregular. Perhaps it's for this reason that there are myriad social media posts dedicated to Hsu's stance in *Stay Gold*. As YouTube user @EE.creative writes, "Jerry Hsu, the true Switch God" – ascribing something divine to a shift in his bodily orientation. @Nirvezz draws us back to earth, acknowledging how a reconfiguration of stance hurts in double: "Take a slam switch stance. it's awkward."

Hsu's switch stance comes with praise not only because of his technical aptitude but also because of the capacity to insert another layer of subjectivity into his somatic behavior. It's about overcoming an injury, as much as it draws attention to the ways we value embodied difference. The few studies done on stance in surfing demonstrate this relationality between the sensory and the social. For instance, sideways movement affects not just the acquisition of athletic techniques, like riding a wave frontside or backside, but also the social pressures for catching specific kinds of waves via sedimented dispositions (cf. Anthony et al. 2016; Furley et al. 2018). In skateboarding, the entanglements between subject formation and athletic techniques are perhaps most tangibly clear by its appreciation of divergent orientations, of the oblique and nonnormative, the uncomfortable, and the gritty.

Feminist writer Sara Ahmed (2006) is interested in what and whom our bodies are oriented by, including what happens when these are not within our immediate reach or feel awkward or are stigmatized. Critiquing phenomenology as a "straightening device," including but not limited to one's sexuality, Ahmed draws attention to the kinds of bodily behavior and sociality less compulsory or proximate. Experiencing bodily disorientation or facing spaces designed for bodies unlike ours, she suggests, drastically affects the way we carry ourselves in the world. Phenomenology foregrounds the processes of smoothening and straightening, aiming to eliminate friction to the point of optimizing one's orientation in the world. More specifically, this means sliding into a hegemonic embodiment, one which is decidedly masculine and heteronormative, and able-bodied and white. "Getting things right," as phenomenologists suggest, often corresponds to ideas of fitting in, of becoming one and universal. Ahmed wonders what happens if we break away from such trodden paths, by way of choice or in line with the core of being:

> The question is not so much finding a queer line but rather asking what our orientation toward queer moments of deviation will be. If the objects slip away, if its face becomes inverted, if it looks odd, strange, or out of place, what will we do?
>
> (2006: 179)

Can such a queer phenomenology be helpful to deepening our understanding of the skater's body – and its stance? Skating switch is a way to make things prick and sting, to render a veiled dominant social order of the senses visible. And there's beauty to this. As YouTube user @mchlselects writes in their appraisal of Hsu's video part, "fuuuck that switch heel down the double set was a poem" (Miner 2011). But, as Ahmed writes, nonnormative bodily orientations face contestation, too. Multiple YouTube commenters draw problematic connections between Hsu's athleticism and ethnicity: "How the fuck he still alive after all those gnarly bails? Was he in Yakuza before" (@m47kr2nt0n in Miner 2011). Or: "i would love to hear the 911 call from someone who lived nearby... hi yes, 911, there is a crazy chinaman, maybe japanese, playing with a skateboard and yelling at a fence" (BigSirZebras in Miner 2011). The nonconformity of skating switch is here confounded with the ethnic categorization of the non-white body – using Asian stereotypes to "praise" Hsu.

As much as the history of skateboarding is one of racial diversity, its discourse reproduces existing power relations (cf. Williams 2020; Willing and Pappalardo 2023). Stance, here, exceeds its position of context-less technical ability. Its sensory pains and pleasures decidedly intersect with normative models of sociality and identity. Learning to skate, let alone attuning to a switch stance, is by no means a universalist experience. What feels most natural or appropriate to some may appear deviant or out of line for others. In *Stay Gold*, Hsu is praised for taking falls like a "Yakuza" or performing tricks as a "Chinaman" or "Japanese." Such readings unmistakably position the white skater's body as a neutral position. Elsewhere, Hsu reads out comments on his skating, saying: "The internet brings out the worst in people. It brings out, like, their most racist thoughts" (Crailtap 2013). He chronicles not only how he's often confused with other skaters of Asian backgrounds but also how his ethnicity is portrayed as representative of "commitment," "being smart," and "being good at everything."

On a panel discussion at Slow Impact (2023), Hsu shared how he wanted to break away from such narratives, seeking to navigate what it means to him to be a child of immigrants. Speaking on both his skate and art practice, he states:

> Perfectionism is all that I understood. 'Cause of the culture I come from, you know, perfectionism is sort of really hammered into you […] If you just look at Chinese characters, just like the amount they have to practice it, to make it absolutely … to turn you to a machine, is sort of the culture I come from. So, a lot of what I do in my life is unconsciously and consciously trying to reject that.

Jerry Hsu's performance in *Stay Gold* shows that each sensory input is an unwitting social stance. Skating switch, here, is a skate technique enveloped in a discourse of racialized stereotypes, gazed upon from a "space of whiteness" (Williams 2022). Put differently: if enskilment is a way for skaters to find their place in the world, this exceeds the immediacy of perception and physical aptitude. This echoes misogynist expressions of skating or running or throwing "like a girl," which "reflect their subordinate position in patriarchal societies and expected gender behavior" (Rana 2022: 294). Bodily performance is legitimized or rejected through sedimented socio-cultural lenses, drawing attention to the kinds of bodies deemed normative and desirable, or unfamiliar and oppositional. An inquiry into the diversity of stance, then, offers a crucial insight into the ways in which the senses are socially modeled, historically formed, and culturally configured (Harris 2020).

The skater's senses

Foregrounding stance is, perhaps surprisingly, not a common practice within skate studies. Most scholarly attention goes to the skater's eye: the capacity to scout "architecture not for historical, symbolic or authorial content but for how surfaces present themselves as skateable surfaces" (Borden 2001a: 219). In this analysis, the urban infrastructure of curbs, stairs, and handrails becomes desirable because of its seemingly limitless potential for play (Vivoni 2009). To skaters, architectural historian Iain Borden intimates, granite, steel, and asphalt present themselves as urban layers of creative density. Aptly conceptualized as the "skater's eye," what's at stake is a mutually transformative encounter between body, tool, and environment (cf. Borden 2001a; Hölsgens 2024).

The mythology of the skater's eye took off around the time that skateboarding moved from emptied swimming pools in the 1970s to the streets in the 1980s. This cultural shift was materially symbolized by the ollie, a tactic of jumping with the board beneath one's feet. The ollie accounts for much of the creativity we observe today, becoming essential to the processes of urban place-making. What exactly is the skater's eye, its gaze and related stance position? Whose eye are we witnessing, and how does it speak to societal orderings of sports and lifestyle, or the cultural tenets of the senses? How can we best capture the entanglements between bodies and spaces? In short, what are the divergent and coinciding subjectivities of skaters?

In a 1987 issue of *Thrasher Magazine*, surf and skate photographer Don Redondo writes a fictional story chronicling how "an average person" loses their sight and surgically implants an eyeball from a dead skater. This eyeball takes on a life of its own, gazing long at curbs and stairs, forcing its new user to divert their attention to their architectural surroundings in a way only a skater would: "She found herself staring at painted curbs and looking for small things to jump 'on' or over" (Redondo 1987: 70). This cyborgian implantation of the all-seeing eye is as much cultural lore as it romanticizes a skate cosmology. Symbolically represented by a green-blue retina, here's a potent tale making the case that skaters universally share a *vision*, a literal worldview. What's more, the skater's eye is hierarchically positioned in relation to the layperson's vision, engendering it desirable and enchanting, as if it renders the world anew. For a moment, the story's protagonist becomes "cross-eyed," seeing two distinct landscapes – one tailored to pedestrian lines of movement and the other to skateable space. Slowly but surely, a paradigm shift unfolds, where she *becomes* a skater, her sight representing a worldview unfamiliar to other city users.

Urban historian Iain Borden takes Redondo's story as a reference point for conceptualizing how skaters navigate the built environment. They do see the city as a site for play, considering space as "a uniform entity" that is "reduced to the homogeneous level of skateable terrain" (Borden 2001b: 13). Over time, this insight is worn out to a commonplace: speak to a skater in the streets and they will comment on how they see the city differently, recognizing creative potential in everyday street furniture. Borden's analysis centers on adolescent boys and young men in the US and UK, who traverse the modernist plazas built by architects like Mies van der Rohe to perform a critique on capitalist rhythms of the city. Despite this situated analysis, Borden's conceptualization of the skater's eye has generated the misconception that all skaters across the globe, no matter their backgrounds or upbringings or beliefs or bodies, and regardless of their spatial surroundings, possess the same kind of vision.

Countering the resulting ocularcentrism in skate studies, there is value to elucidating such a singular cyborg ontology by modeling a "skater's ear." Following Don Redondo, a collective of skate scholars ask their readers to imagine an ear transplant patient receiving the aurality of a dead skater:

> As she walks back to her flat, she hears a rattle sound, a grind, and a set of cheers. Part of her is annoyed, while another part of her dances sideways in celebration. It is as if the sounds of skateboarding transport her to their cause, extending her mind to an activity that unlocks a knowledge of the city previously unknown.
> (Glenney et al. forthcoming).

This aural knowledge is prompted by a theory of texturology, an episteme of the city that uses the vibrations of sound for knowing the ground: the material surfaces reverberate in the skater's body and, in so doing, co-produce the potential for emplaced creativity (Glenney et al. forthcoming). As skilled listeners, they aurally perceive the inner-workings of their ball bearings, the snapiness of their wooden plank, the skateability of an obstacle, the antisociality of the obstacle's protectors – the police – and the sociality of their peers. These skatesounds act as social invites to friendly peers, while also betraying their presence to surveying security. As such, skateboarding holds an acoustemological potentiality, pointing to "what is knowable and how it becomes known through sounding and listening to that which is audible" (Littlejohn 2021: 40). To the informed ear, the gritty sonic matter of polyurethane wheels is an indexical sign of an emphatically wanted or unwanted presence: a sonic awareness of the not-yet-seen.

Might smell and taste contribute to this multisensory array, including bodily fluids such as sweat and blood enmeshed with alleyway funk of urban

The Skater's Body 23

Figure 2.2 Ruby Lilley taking off her skate shoes after jumping into a pool, having lost a bet.

Source: Photo by Taylor Ballard.

pollution? Does the riskiness of skateboarding's exploits add to this sensory array, perhaps paralleling the feeling of vertigo, similar to that of highwire walking? Stanced activities like skateboarding are not merely visual, nor aural, but embodied, pointing toward the uninterrupted reciprocity between the body and its environs. Pao Nowodworski (2023) connects the skater's sensorium with the vestibular sense – equilibrioception, or the perception of balance and spatial awareness. He reasons that the sense of balance, located in an organ in the middle ear, plays a crucial role in sideways movement: the vestibular is coupled with vision to produce a communal gaze, a multisensory endeavor that includes the imagination of a trick performed at a designated spot.

Becoming a skater

Adding a multisensorial addendum to Don Redondo's story is insightful for understanding how people learn to skate. But the most pressing issue is that these cumulative readings often assume that sensory models are universal, as if enskilment transpires in the same way to all skaters. However, the fictional origins of the skater's eye already confirm that a universalist understanding of its techniques is not tenable. The skater who dies is a man, whose driver's license has expired and whose soul floats away "on to better things." The cyborgian eye transplant is performed on a young woman, living at her mom's. Her daytime gaze at skateable space translates into nightmares, in which she speeds "down a big black asphalt hill, not in a car or anything, but way too fast" (Redondo 1987: 71). For the deceased skater, Redondo notes, such speeds are like a "good song," unbelievable yet thrilling and full of flow, but not for the woman: she is frightened by the skater's gaze, requiring the visit of a doctor to check in on her.

The gender typology of both protagonists shouldn't be seen as a coincidence: what's at stake is an archetypal story of the supposed masculine desire and feminine fear of danger, velocity, and adventure. Rather than an enmeshment of stance and ethnicity, as is the case in the popular discourse on Jerry Hsu's video, sight is here a punctuating device for a decidedly gendered orientation. It's important to note that Redondo's story is published in a core skate magazine, *Thrasher*. These media outlets have a legacy of featuring rugged "men who are skilled and risk-taking," while framing "women in sexualized ways or as less skilled" (Beal and Ebeling 2019: 105). The skater's eye, portrayed in this mediated context, takes on a male gaze, drawing attention to narratives of assimilation. The story's protagonist *becomes a skater* by acquiring a man's eye rather than through situated learning and enskilment. What's more, the skater's ability to identify skateable space is deemed undesirable or even unhealthy for nonnormative skaters: her mother suggests seeing a doctor, as if such techniques do not belong to a woman's body.

Challenging these gendered models of the skater's gaze and ocularcentrism, artist-researcher Dani Abulhawa (2020) stresses that skateboarding's ultimate expression – trick play – can best be categorized as bodily kinesthetic intelligence. She notes how skaters merge a tacit knowledge of one's own motile and sensory perception, the ability to reproduce motion observed in others, and the capacity to precisely execute intentional movements. What emerges is an emplaced interplay between normative and personalized techniques. While most skaters do perform tricks by creatively engaging architecture, this is by no means a universalist form of skill acquisition, nor does it mean that seemingly similar movements feel or mean the same to all. Learning to skate is not a simple matter of acquiring *the* skater's eye and performing tricks accordingly. Rather, it is an enskilment that centers the practitioner's own sense of their embodied self, conditioned by the expectations of others about sensory perception and shaped by the social structures of an environment (Glenney 2023). "The resulting performance," Abulhawa (2020: 72) writes, "may look the same as that produced by another body, but it doesn't mean that both bodies arrive at the trick or indeed that they perform the trick in the same way."

Dutch Olympian Candy Jacobs is intimately aware of the variations of embodied and emplaced experiences, including how these are mediated by social and cultural structures: "If I would jump El Toro [a set of twenty stairs] twice, I would probably tear all my shit up. I know that if [professional skater] Nyjah [Huston] does it five times in a row, he's gonna be good" (Pushing Boarders 2019). Jacobs ascribes this bodily difference to the historical lineage of the skate industry, who have supported men over women and gender-nonconforming people for multiple decades. Such industry-wide support resulted in a context where professional athletes like Jacobs had to pay out of their own pocket to get fitness coaches and medical support, limiting the training for high-performance tricks and increasing the socio-economic repercussions of injuries. What's more, Jacobs, skating at El Toro would result in a decidedly different sensory experience and social set of meanings compared to multi-millionaire Nyjah Huston, whose athletic performance is made possible by brands like Nike and Monster. Jacobs expresses how she's achingly familiar with the gendered standard for skating: women and gender nonconforming people must skate like Nyjah Huston, *like a man*, to attract attention from the skate industry. Alternatively, these skaters have to mold themselves to what the industry considers marketable, which generally means attuning to the male gaze (Abulhawa 2020).

At times, systemic adversity results in the reappropriation of claims to proficiency. Sport scientist Åsa Bäckström (2013) discusses a performative resistance by all-women skate networks in Sweden. Taking ownership of discourses of competency and skill to perform resistance through the Swedish word *grym*, loosely translated as "cruel and awesome," the network claims prowess and ability in a male-dominated community. As such, they legitimize their presence, not least by reappropriating a terminology otherwise associated with a masculine sway of pride and power. These skaters perform a social stance by reappropriating a gendered norm. Simultaneously, an increasing number of elite mature skaters (supported by sports and health brands) now advertise their use of diet plans, workout regimes, and sobriety advocacy to non-professional skaters. By promoting an *athletic* lifestyle, rather than one rooted in urban and street culture, these skaters pivot on health and wellness. Put differently, bodily techniques, like sideways movement, acquire situated meanings in specific contexts – opening up the possibility for subject formation and communal practices.

The point, here, is that the senses are necessarily mediated by encultured socialities like gender, providing a critique of gestalt and early phenomenological ideas that claim immediate, unfiltered, and primordial embodied perception. As sensory anthropologist, David Howes (2023: 154) writes,

> social factors, therefore, along with individual abilities and environmental allowances, deeply influence our mode of seeing, hearing, smelling, and so on. To assert otherwise is not merely an act of gross naïveté; it is a sign of contempt for the ways in which individuals and social groups have had their senses constrained and their experiences disdained by the politics of perception put forward by the dominant class.

Building upon this foundational insight from the anthropology of the senses, we must account for the contextual peculiarities of the skater's sensorium, i.e. how the senses are ordered, tuned, and integrated. This is further complicated by the recognition that skaters hold divergent, at times hierarchically organized social positions (Dupont 2014): filmers and photographers can visually identify skateable space and test their textural sounds with incredible acuity, tasked with visually and sonically recording these performances. Spotters position themselves on the sidewalks and streets to prevent skaters from crashing into pedestrians and vehicles, combining a tacit knowledge of urban rhythms with an intimate familiarity with trick play. The skaters performing the tricks have an attuned vestibular and textural sensory array that can pick out the "feel" of a spot, imagining potential stanced bodily movements as enhanced by their tool, the skateboard.

Becoming a skater – including the process of learning to skate switch or habituating the skater's dominant sensory modes – is located at the axes of class, ethnicity, gender, access, and ability. Marginalized populations of skaters cannot necessarily run the risk of being arrested for their illegal play or using abandoned city spaces, reinforcing that the mythologized skater's eye is a decidedly white and male organ (cf. Abulhawa 2020; Williams 2020). Besides, the skater's eye plays out distinctly among skaters with divergent eye conditions, some of whom use a white cane during trick performances – foregrounding tactility and sonic practices for proprioception (Carroll and Cianciotto 2020). Sensorially, the vibrations of wheels on street surfaces can strike neurodiverse bodies in a more aggressive fashion, enmeshing tingling joy with overwhelming stimuli, a misophonia. From trick play and sideways orientation to urban place-making and athletic performance, a skater's stance envelops the sensory and the social.

Note

1 Parts of this section are derived from or revised reflections on Hölsgens' PhD thesis, *A Phenomenology of Skateboarding in Seoul, South Korea: Experiential and filmic observations* (2018), made open access as *Skateboarding in Seoul: A Sensory Ethnography* (2021).

References

Abulhawa, D. (2020). *Skateboarding and Femininity: Gender, Space-Making and Expressive Movement*. London: Routledge.

Ahmed, S. (2006). "Orientations: Toward a Queer Phenomenology." *GLQ: A Journal of Lesbian and Gay Studies*, 12.4: 543–574.

Alexandre, M.. (2023). "Skateboarding Stance and Handedness: A Brief Analysis of Relationship, Proportions and Influences." *arXiv* preprint arXiv:2310.11460.

Anthony, C., Brown, L., Coburn, J., Galpin, A. J., & Tran, T. T. (2016). "Stance Affects Balance in Surfers." *International Journal of Sports Science & Coaching*, 11: 446–450.

Bäckström, Å (2013). "Gender Manoeuvring in Swedish Skateboarding: Negotiations of Femininities and the Hierarchical Gender Structure." *Young*, 21.1: 29–53.

Beal, B., & Ebeling, K. (2019). "Can You Sell Out if You've Never Been in? The Olympics and Creating Spaces for Gender Inclusion in Skateboarding." In Schwier, J., & Kilberth, V. (eds.). *Skateboarding between Subculture and Olympics*, 97–116. Bielefeld: Transcript.

Blakely, J. (2014). *Surf's Up in Rare Books. Smithsonian*, https://blog.library.si.edu/blog/2014/07/02/surfs-up-in-rare-books/.

Borden, I. (2001a). *Skateboarding, Space and the City: Architecture and the Body*. Oxford: Berg Publishers.

Borden, I. (2001b). "Another Pavement, Another Beach: Skateboarding and the Performative Critique of Architecture." In Borden, I., Kerr, J., & Rendell, J. (eds.). *The Unknown City: Contesting Architecture and Social Space*, 178–199. Cambridge: MIT Press.

Carroll, T., & Cianciotto, L. (2020). "Towards Radical Empathy." In Hölsgens, S. & Callan-Riley, T. (eds.). *Urban Pamphleteer #8 Skateboardings*, 11–12. London: UCL Urban Laboratory

Crailtap. (2013). *Crailtap's We Shred It, You Said It, We Read It with Jerry Hsu*, 14 April 2023, https://www.youtube.com/watch?v=H6P7OQyy5Eg.

Davidson, B. (1976). *The Skateboard Book*. New York: Grosset and Dunlap.

Desjarlais, R., & Jason Throop, C. (2011). "Phenomenological Approaches in Anthropology." *Annual Review of Anthropology*, 40: 87–102.

Dupont, T. (2014). "From core to Consumer: The Informal Hierarchy of the Skateboard Scene." *Journal of Contemporary Ethnography*, 43.5: 556–581.

Furley, P., Dörr, J., & Loffing, F. (2018). "Goofy vs. Regular: Laterality Effects in Surfing." *Laterality*, 23.6: 629–642.

Glenney, B. (2023). "Polluted Leisure Enskilment: Skateboarding as Ecosophy." *Leisure Sciences*, 2023: 1–25.

Glenney, B., Boutin, M., & O'Connor, P. (Forthcoming). "The Skater's Ear: A Sensuous Complexity of Skateboarding Sound." *Sport and Society*.

Gowlland, G. (2019). "The Sociality of Enskilment." *Ethnos*, 84.3: 508–524.

Harris, A. (2020). *A Sensory Education*. London: Routledge.

Heidegger, M. (1927[1962]). *Being and Time*. Transl. John Macquarrie and Edward Robinson. New York: Harper & Row.

Hölsgens, S. (2018). *A Phenomenology of Skateboarding in Seoul, South Korea: Experiential and Filmic Observations*. UCL: PhD Thesis.

Hölsgens, S. (2021). *Skateboarding in Seoul: A Sensory Ethnography*. Groningen: University of Groningen Press.

Hölsgens, S. (2024). "Learning to See or How to Make Sense of the Skillful Things Skateboarders Do." In Vannini, P. (ed.). *The Routledge International Handbook of Sensory Ethnography*, 387–400. New York: Routledge.

Hough-Snee, D. Z., & Eastman, A. S. (eds.) (2017). *The Critical Surf Studies Reader*. Durham: Duke University Press.

Howes, D. (2023). *Sensorial Investigations: A History of the Senses in Anthropology, Psychology, and Law*. Pennsylvania: Penn State University Press.

Ingold, T. (2000). *The Perception of the Environment: Essays on Livelihood, Dwelling and Skill*. London: Taylor & Francis Group.

Littlejohn, A. (2021). "Sonic Ethnography." In Grasseni, C., Barendregt, B., De Maaker, E., De Musso, F., Littlejohn, A., Maeckelbergh, M., Postma, M., & Westmoreland, M. (eds.). *Audiovisual and Digital Ethnography*, 35–60. London: Routledge.

Loland, S., & Bäckström, Å (2023). "Into the Glidescape: An Outline of Gliding Sports from the Perspective of Applied Phenomenology." *Journal of the Philosophy of Sport*, 50.3: 365–382.

Merleau-Ponty, M. (1945[2013]). *Phenomenology of Perception*. New York: Routledge.

Miner, J. (2010). *Emerica Presents: Stay Gold*, https://www.youtube.com/watch?v=gWTg4WzrWqc.

Miner, J. (2011). *Emerica Presents: Emerica Stay Gold B-Side: Jerry Hsu*, https://www.youtube.com/watch?v=jMFdQP3v3wY&.

Moser, P. (2008). *Pacific Passages: An Anthology of Surf Writing*. Honolulu: University of Hawaii Press.

Muirhead, D. (1962). *Surfing in Hawaii: A Personal Memoir*. Crosslake: Northland Press.

Nootens, N., & Harrison-Caldwell, M. (2017). "What Determines Your Skate Stance?" *Jenkem Magazine*, 12 October 2017, https://www.jenkemmag.com/home/2017/10/12/determines-skate-stance/.

Nowodworski, P. (2023). "Balance as a skater's Duty? Sensual-Trained Action as an Expression of Scene Affiliation in Skateboarding." In Eisewicht, P., Hitzler, R., & Schäfer, L. (eds.). *The Social Meaning of the Senses: The Reconstruction of Sensory Aspects of Knowledge*, 99–116. Wiesbaden: Springer Fachmedien Wiesbaden.

Pálsson, G. (1994). "Enskilment at Sea." *Man*, 29.4: 901–927.

Rana, J. (2022). "Gendered Enskilment: Becoming Women through Recreational Running." *The Senses and Society*, 17.3: 290–302.

Redondo, D. (1987). "The Skater's Eye." *Thrasher Magazine*, September 1987: 70–71.

Slow Impact. (2023). *Empathy And Texture*, 8 March 2023, https://www.youtube.com/watch?v=WXbdaFShcn0.

Vivoni, F. (2009). "Spots of Spatial Desire: Skateparks, Skateplazas, and Urban Politics." *Journal of Sport and Social Issues*, 33.2: 130–49.

Whiteley, M. (2015). "Chrome Ball Interview #84: jerry hsu." *Chrome ball*, https://chromeballincident.blogspot.com/2015/09/chrome-ball-interview-84-jerry-hsu.html.

Williams, N. (2020). *Colour in the Lines: The Racial Politics and Possibilities of US Skateboarding Culture*. PhD thesis: University of Waikato.

Williams, N. (2022). "Before the Gold: Connecting Aspirations, Activism, and BIPOC Excellence through Olympic Skateboarding." *Journal of Olympic Studies*, 3.1: 4–27.

Willing, I., & Pappalardo, A. (2023). *Skateboarding, Power and Change*. Berlin: Springer.

Woods, C.T., Rudd, J., Gray, R., & Davids, K. (2021). "Enskilment: An Ecological-Anthropological Worldview of Skill, Learning and Education in Sport." *Sports Medicine-Open*, 7.1: 1–9.

3 Crafting the City
Embodied, Symbolic, and Engaged Skateboarding

"What does it mean," architectural historian Jane Rendell (2007: 187) asks, "to write a site that one has not visited, that can only be imagined, to know a place not with your feet, but with your eyes tracing lines on a map, words in a sentence, dots on a screen?" Ask skaters, we suggest. They have the capacity to describe a site unvisited based on their engagement with hours upon hours of their peers' audiovisual recordings (Hölsgens 2021). By facing skate imagery on a daily basis, they have a second-hand understanding of skateable space across the globe. Its textured skin, sonic resonance, and social configuration are imagined, considered, and even experienced in an active process of spectatorship: the video is a representation of a sensorium as much as it is a sensuous subject as and of itself (Sobchack 1992). These recordings exceed the plain role of communication by foregrounding a mimetic means of sensing the empirical world: the skater's eye and ear are extended into the virtual, offering an experiential resource to sense what a site might look, sound, feel, and smell like.

Familiarizing oneself with someone else's worldview through mere *dots on a screen* means going beyond the immediacy of one's own sensorial experience. What's conveyed through film is the socio-materiality of a site, fostering "a contact between perceiver and object represented [...] as though one were touching a film with one's own eyes" (Marks 2000: xi). For film scholar Laura Marks, this point of contact transforms or even pollutes "viewers' ideas of cultural distinction, implicating each of us in them" (idem: xii). The intercultural circulation of videos engenders a continuous dialogue between site-specific skate communities – like exponentially growing chain letters. Collectively, skaters and spectators craft a discourse of skateable space, building a heritage for the skate-minded senses.

Not unlike the Situationists' notion of psychogeography and graffiti artists' use of tags, skaters combine the analytic and associative to scrutinize *and* socially transform the built environment. This is articulated through the emic notion of a *spot*: a site identified, appreciated, and bolstered for its skateability. Similar to how human geographers and architectural historians differentiate between abstract space and the tangibility of lived-in places, skaters

DOI: 10.4324/9781003510642-3
This chapter has been made available under a CC-BY-NC-ND 4.0 license.

contrast the openness of the streets to the peculiar signification of spots. The latter are microhabitats, usually a few square feet in size, and regularly unrecognized by non-skaters as a site of meaning.

Their recording devices are by no means neutral or observant, either: the community's acclaim of handheld cameras, fisheye lenses, and cardioid microphones is full of sensoriality and theoretical prefiguration, capturing in image and sound what they seek to find in the city. As much as skaters learn to sense skateable space through armchair methods, not least by scrolling through social media feeds, their relationality to their surroundings is decidedly mediated *and* emplaced: watching videos at home and moving sideways in public spaces are mutually transformative. As film scholar Jenny Chamarette (2012: 66) suggests, "cinema cannot be solely a representational system; it is as much a mode of embodied gestures as it is a system of relational signs […] The sense-making of the cinema is also world-making of me, and my sensing body." These seemingly distinct modes of sensing – mediated and immediate – blend together, resulting in a patchwork sensory model used for trick play. This sensuous enskilment of mediated play exists in a decidedly socio-spatial reality: its somatics and performativity exist by the grace of the built environment. That is the topic of this chapter: how skaters use their senses to craft both nondescript spaces and famed architecture into *skate spots*, inserting socio-historical meaning onto the pragmatic surfaces of the cityscape.

Figure 3.1 Helena Long, Una Farrar, and Shari White scouting for skate spots in Malmö.

Source: Photo by Norma Ibarra.

Crafting space

Anthropologist Tim Ingold (2004) remarks how the hardness of city streets, designed to resist the marks of feet, deletes any track-record of passage. Paths of desire, an urban taboo formed by walking on green spaces, are instances of defacement, not enhancement – considered a subversive threat: "Green spaces are for looking at, not for walking on; reserved for visual contemplation rather than for exploration on foot" (Ingold 2004: 329). But skaters do explore and leave their mark on the built environment, whether it be material scratches or social subversions. Skaters are thus a double subversion, interrupting the rhythmic flow of pedestrians and vehicles, while also leaving their unwanted marks on curbs, ledges, handrails, and any other surfaces they find accessible and desirable. Their toes and heels acquire the urban topography in their pushing craft: their toes are an epistemological contact point for the textures of the built environment, while their heels dampen the irregularities of the city's horizontal surfaces. For the pedestrian, Ingold suggests, these surfaces are an unknown known: the most used but the least felt – a commonplace unfamiliar. But to the skater, these are known through a multisensorial feedback loop.

Skaters are wheeled threats on the sidewalks that can compete with cars in the street. Their mobility follows a socially adept movement that involves complex and constant sensorial scanning of material surfaces and social obstacles. Going at a faster pace on a vehicle more susceptible to sudden pebble-based stops with a squirrely center of gravity, they must constantly have a diagrammatic awareness of the ground, while also surveying pedestrians around them, looking in their eyes to read their potential directional shifts, responses of fear and anger, and abrupt movements of their pet dogs. But the skater and pedestrian are in the city with different intentions, distinct sensoriums, and diverging techniques. The skater knows the sensorial reflexes of the pedestrian, while the pedestrian habitually fears the skater. Skate sounds, here, act as indicators for unavoidable collision and frustrated wayfinding.

Rather than cobblestones or patchwork roads, modern cities are marked by smooth surfaces and automotive infrastructures – characteristics of the global advent of paved paradises (Grabar 2023). Abandoned alleyways, undercrofts, and bridges are common spaces for play, exploration, and joy, at times alongside other socially rejected activities like drug abuse, homelessness, and sex work (cf. Cianciotto 2020; Woolley and Johns 2001). Skateboarding flourishes because of these architectural typologies: urban planning prioritizing wheeled transportation and capitalist modes of transaction frequently befalls cruising around on a skateboard. Similarly, functionalist design tailored to median human scale (including handrails, staircases, and benches) has historically coincided with trick performance, not least because of its standardized measurement systems: once a trick is learned on one handrail, it can be fairly easily transferred to another.

These navigational strategies are often learned through peer-apprenticeship and informal learning strategies. It may be possible to consider other aspects of skateboarding anew in the context of craft. What is it to observe skateboarding through a craft lens and position it alongside wooden boat building, gardening, and cooking in its sociality, place-making, do-it-yourself (DIY) ethos, and skill expertise (Sennett 2008; Watson and Shove 2008)? In the field of anthropology, there is a wide and deep discourse of craft learning akin to skateboarding – specifically in the context of tool use, from making boats (Malinowski (1922[2014]) to weaving baskets (Boas 1927[1955]). More recently, Tim Ingold (2000: 407) positioned crafts as a poetics of tool use, zooming in on tool- and object-specific activities we engage in "without attending to them *as such.*" Experts perform craftsmanship intuitively: they simply craft or make or play.

This intuitive crafting applies to skateboarding most clearly through its spontaneous scouting for space affording the performance of tricks: skaters use the skateboard as a tool to navigate the city. Their tool use? Rendering regular street furniture *skateable*, a skill that is more narrowly understood as "soft." As a technologically literate community, skaters-as-artisans experience the skateboard as an extension of their body, an instrument enabling the execution of skillful tricks – parallel to a hammer befitting the craftsmanship of making furniture (Hölsgens 2018). Like other types of craftsmanship, skateboarding is not just about the succession of technical procedures. Rather, and following Geoffrey Gowlland's (2015: 287) anthropological understanding of craft techniques, it is a type of crafting involving the "anticipation of the next operation in a fluid performance." What's at stake is a pedagogy of noticing *in situ*, an attention tailored to praxis and experience rather than technicalities or mechanical procedures. Sensory ethnographer Tom Martin (2021: 15) sees this craftsmanship as a perceptual transformation, learning "to perceive details in objects that had previously been invisible." Perhaps, then, skateboarding is more a craft than a sport. More precisely, it presses close to being a craft *of* the modern city.

Consider a common scene, a "hand rail battle," an aptly titled video by Yoshiaki Toeda (2024). Set in a nondescript public park, we see a handrail running parallel to the pitch of stairs. The hardpan surface of the park's terrain is crusty and coarse, supplying sufficient grip for pedestrians and cyclists. For skaters, such asphalt offers a challenge: their small, polyurethane wheels struggle to gain traction on grippy textures. We see Nanaka Fujisawa and Wakyo Sakamoto, two acclaimed Japanese skaters. While sharing a skate session, they focus on different tricks, cheering each other on after each failed attempt. An observant spectator will notice a third person in the frame: Anthony Claravall, a photographer and videographer whose work has been at the forefront of skate media since his contributions to 411VM in the 1990s (Roberts 2021).

What unfolds is a triangle of action. Fujisawa and Sakamoto take turns, each of whom stanced goofy yet arrival at the handrail from different angles and gendered orientations (Chapter 2). Between each turn, Claravall must also change his perspective, ensuring his photographs capture not only the swift movements of Fujisawa and Sakamoto skaters' feet but also their emotive facial expressions from the front. And then there is Yoshiaki Toeda, who films this rhythm of play and image-making. For minutes on end, we see both skaters fall and tumble. Fujisawa's pristine white t-shirt gets filthier with each attempt – progressively imprinted with the brown-grey traces of the crusty terrain. Concurrently, similar imprints start to emerge on her hands, which repeatedly catch falls and smack into the hardpan surfaces of the asphalt. Fujisawa's "hand rail battle"? Landing a pop shuvit to fifty-fifty – a highly technical and awkward trick. As YouTube user @ManuelOpeinso comments, "Pop shuv to 50 down a handrail is soooo fucking scary. The commitment to grind this one out is huge … good shit."

After twenty-six attempts, Fujisawa manages to land the trick, after which all present run up to her for a shared celebration. Showing her bloodied hand and shirt to the camera, Fujisawa is acutely aware of the repercussions of her actions: this battle came at the expense of potentially ruined attire and skin-deep wounds – a skater's embodiment commonly associated with hegemonic masculinity (Beal and Ebeling 2019). Or, as user @yahngtoonzentertainment4470 ironically states, "I had to call out at work today because I was in so much pain just from watching. She has my respect." Thanking videographer Toeda, she then turns to Claravall – who shows her a sample of the pictures taken. Seeing what she's landed, her joyful smile turns to laughter while she exclaims, *yokatta!* ("I'm glad/that was good!").

Nanaka Fujisawa's skilled vision is her capacity to notice creative potential in a seemingly nondescript park. This modeling of the senses is at once tailored to her emplaced technique and shared with her peers: photographer Claravall and videographer Toeda are attuned to her bodily movements, intuitively using their recording devices to capture her creativity. The crew uses their subjective and overlapping bodily techniques to insert meaning onto the nonplace of an urban park, crafting meaning out of a nonplace. By identifying skateable space and transforming it into an aesthetic device for play, Fujisawa increases her capital within the skate community (D'Orazio 2020). But why? What is it about steel handrails, grippy asphalt, and stairs that prompt a craft-like assemblage of creativity? It is to these questions that we now turn.

Heel knowledge

"Great cities are not made by automobiles, freeways and high rises. Basically, they are made by open spaces and the people who use the open spaces" (Halprin in Kale 2016). Lawrence Halprin's urban theory gave way to his own architectural design of open, hardpan plazas throughout urban America of the 1970s and 1980s. Yet, many of Halprin's brickscaped plazas quickly became decrepit, lifeless dead spaces, seemingly *too* open and *too* hard. The Water Garden, Skyline Park, and the Sculpture Garden all denote natural biota in name but lacked any biodiversity around which people wish to gather. Some plazas were greenified over time, a move that he likened to sketching a mustache on Mona Lisa (Lelchuk 2003).

Though Halprin's urban designs failed to get people out of the comfort of their offices, diners, or yarded suburb-scapes (Soltz 2016), they enlivened a growing population of youth equipped with a faddish wheeled tool: skateboards. By the late 1980s, the entirety of San Francisco's Herman Plaza, dubbed "EMB" by skaters, became a testing ground for street skating. Here, too, greens were lacking, though there exist virtual biota: massive steel waterfall sculptures and concrete wave-forms that emulated the sea, doubling as a sound barrier for the intervening freeway. Spatially, EMB includes a wrap of small staircases, a waterfall of stepped ledges, and above all smooth bricks. Here, the microhabitats of curbs and ledges coincide with the monumental quality of landscape architecture. What is it about sites of modernity like these that speaks to the skater's sensorium?

"A skatepark is to a McChicken Sandwich as a spot is to a Carne Asada Burrito wet with red sauce," asserts Felix Soto.[1] A Los Angeles-based filmer for Baker Skateboards, Felix has identified and documented hundreds, if not thousands, of skate spots. "My favorite spot is EMB. The whole aesthetic is so beautiful: the sound, the people, it's got just the right taste. It's always fresh." The multisensorial imaginary of space shifted skate culture from emptied pools, schoolyards, and sidewalks to a more public decorum. Speaking to his local spots in his hometown of Los Angeles, Felix describes the importance of tuning spot to skater, and vice versa: "I try to find a spot that fits my aesthetic and the skater. Schoolyards are usually stale, but the streets and sidewalks never are. Even a house spot [connected to domestic infrastructures, including handrails or roofs] always lands into a sidewalk." Felix's sensory metaphor of taste to describe a spot, as "fresh" or "stale," presents a tuning of his sensorium. The meshwork of skateparks is largely pre-ordained by their design: skateparks are mass-produced and skating them is, to Felix, like a fast-food experience, where creativity falls flat. Streets and sidewalks, by contrast, lack pre-ordained performativity: street spaces are like a street truck burrito, always fresh.

Felix's spot know-how is a social act as much as it is a physical act insofar as it contributes to a network of space, obstacles, and people. Other thinkers, including anthropologist Bruno Latour (2005: 177), liken such a network to a spider on a web, knowing their prey has landed by feeling the web's vibrations. So too, Felix's engagement with a spot like EMB is caught in a skate space's web, picking up the vibrations of other activities that shake the web like stuck prey. Felix knows Los Angeles' web-like meshwork through its skate-infused vibrations. When asked to describe the specific material attributes of what makes a good spot, Felix pauses for around ten seconds, and then awkwardly said, "imagine." Then, after another long pause, he concludes, "I'm kinda fried right now, I guess."

When plied further for specific spatial features that make for a good site, Felix remains silent. This has nothing to do with a lack of knowing. Felix is a well-informed skate spotter and purveyor in Los Angeles, celebrated across

Southern California. If anything, his silence is an indicator of his embodied knowledge, his *city craft*. An enskiled knower can never match their adept skill with discursive language: finding and using spots is a bodily technique reflecting a deep and integrated existence in the world. It is difficult to speak about one's own techniques when they are enmeshed in one's sensorial engagement with the world. Rather, the judgment of curbs and ledges and stairs and rails reside as know-how, in the heel not the head.

A spot typology

Skaters have a catalog knowledge of spots: they know which tricks were performed, when, and by whom. In an interview for skate platform Quartersnacks (Golding 2024, online), professional skater Ben Kadow exemplifies how a spot is made and remade – discussing a famed skate spot in New York City, "The Blubba," a marble ledge down several steps. Kadow shares his admiration of Anthony Pappalardo's trick play, regularly celebrated for its originality and creativity:

> [T]hat's my favorite trick probably out of everything Pappalardo has done: the ollie into Black Hubba. That blew my mind, I was like, 'This is how I'm going to skate now.' It's a classic spot, everyone skated the main hubba, and he went off to the side and did that. It's two handrails going down each side and he threads the needle at the end. I thought that was so cool.
>
> If a part has mostly New York clips in it, then [it's] an easy one to like, but the funny thing is that growing up, I'd seen Pappalardo video parts, but I never really appreciated them. *Fully Flared* [and *Homeboy*] was him taking a different route in his approach to skating and it really struck a chord with me. It was the first time I understood how impactful simple tricks on cool spots could be. That really resonated with me; it changed my outlook.

To Kadow, the "ollie from the side" reveals that the Blubba exceeds its status as a material object. It has a socio-temporal history. Contrary to most skaters grinding down the ledge, Pappalardo crafted the spot into something anew, approaching it sideways. Maneuvering in between two handrails and a lamppost, there's myriad room for error: he should crash into one of these obstacles but somehow goes around them. The performance itself – an ollie – is hardly original. Its creative power is its negativity: rather than performing an obstacle-based trick, Anthony Pappalardo expresses his bodily techniques by attending to the spot's negative or empty space. Like a figure-ground reversal, his creativity is rendering unseen space visible for play. Adding an aesthetic and performative layer of sense-making to the historical meshwork of the Blubba, Pappalardo defamiliarizes the familiar in a way that subverts its standard socio-spatial meaning of skateability. This sensorial attunement to negative space reconfigures how Ben Kadow thinks of his own skate craft: "That really resonated with me; it changed my outlook."

The audiovisual recording of the Blubba's negative space – symbolically represented through Pappalardo's ollie – engenders an intersubjective and emplaced spectatorship. It is as much an expression of Pappalardo's enculturation of the senses as it points to a transformative enskilment for its spectators, including Ben Kadow. The represented object resounds in the spectator's subjective body, resulting in an enactive and participatory mode of spectatorship. As Laura Marks (2000: 48) writes, "If a viewer is free to draw upon her own reserves of memory as she participates in the creation of the object on screen, her private and unofficial histories and memories will be granted as much legitimation as the official histories that make up the regime of the cliché – if not more." It is the mutually reinforcing interplay between Pappalardo's ollie and Kadow's spectatorship that turns Blubba into a socio-spatial meshwork. What they leave behind are traces of (recorded) creativity to some or deviant debris to others (Dickinson et al. 2022). By crafting a spot through mediated play, these skaters insert their own aesthetic, politic, and affect onto the hardpan surfaces of the built environment – unsettling and remaking the geographical tendencies of the modernist city.

A spot is not static; it's alive. It is an idealized refuge affording creative and transgressive modes of being, plied by the skater's apparatus to indiscriminately discover and exploit. A spot is as material as it is socio-historical, from which it becomes a point of departure, an opening, "a line of becoming" (Deleuze and Guattari 1987). Similarly, a skate video is not just an indexical registration of tricks: it operates as a sensorial point of contact between skaters, spectator, and spot, cultivating skin-deep entanglements between image and body (Hölsgens 2024). Considering a skate spot as a social construct departs from the view that they are unveiled or discovered: it is constantly made, produced, and crafted, roaring with alternating meanings adding layers across space and time. Spots can be iconic because of their skateability, as much as their location can offer convenience despite their mediocre design. Pulsating with life, they can be fresh or stale, grow in and out of fashion, and well-maintained or fragile. Skaters like Kadow develop situated bodily techniques for noticing these meanings, not unlike ants tracking the trails of their kin. Some of these traces are visible: grinded edges, wax traces, and color alterations are material residue from this spot-making craft. Others, like videographic recordings indiscernible to non-skaters, offer an archeology of an encultured regime of knowledge: a skater's city craft becomes their sensorial signature.

These remnants are a symbol for visiting skaters to imagine *what might have been* or *could be*, as Thom Callan-Riley's PhD project "How beautiful it can be" (unpublished) argues. Skaters sometimes engage architecture through other skaters' bodies: "I see the city differently. But it is not because I can individually and bodily perform the tricks that transform the mundane architecture. I am experiencing the architecture through the embodiment of others."

Existing alongside other use-cases of the city, spots are existentially meaningful, creating a dense and multi-layered network of actors, wherein a skater can become a knowledgeable node (Hölsgens 2021). Their urban expertise results in an ever-growing, nonlinear mental topology of the city – a figuration that is constantly folding and unfolding, becoming anew with each shift in direction. It is for this reason that many skaters will tell you to go to a local skate shop to ask for the best spots, instead of performing a Google search. While you may find some famed spots in the ether of the virtual, the city's best hidden secrets are intentionally poorly documented – at least, in terms of conventional mapping strategies. In part, the obscurity of this topography is because it is exchanged through oral storytelling, never in its entirety and always in diffused wordings. Like a rhizome, spots are dynamic proliferations of roots and offshoots, lacking a clear beginning and end, and instead constantly in the process of becoming (cf. Deleuze and Guattari 1987; Glenney 2023).

At times, camouflaging spots is done on purpose. The unused, abandoned, or illegal status of spots cultivates a spatial desire for their use: a "love for unloved spaces" (O'Connor 2019: 143). For instance, Tyshawn Jones became the 2022 "Thrasher Skater of the Year" by performing a trick at a spot seemingly inaccessible: the gap between two subway tracks. The historical concealment of this site for skateboarding and the elaborate ceremony of the performance elevate the space to a part of skate lore (D'Orazio 2020). This, in turn, gives Jones and his crew a kind of fetishistic power that subsequently endows them with an expert knowledge of their city craft. Skating such spots also includes an experiential shift, as "skaters construct a different temporal rhythm by staying longer in an urban plaza as others hurry through" (Borden 2001: 198). This arrhythmia produces a sensory awareness of capitalism's temporality: skaters sense the whereabouts of security guards and office workers; gauge the flow of cars, cyclists, and pedestrians; and infuse places of labor with an intervention of nonwork.

Once a spot is identified by authorities, it might be constantly surveilled or modified with hostile architecture and skate stoppers, limiting the window of opportunity for uninterrupted play. Tim Sedo (2010: 274) chronicles how avid Chinese skaters are cautious to share their mental map of spots with newcomers: there is a legacy of professional skaters, particularly those from the US (and, increasingly, Europe), who "fly to new countries, skate their spots, and often blow them out" – meaning they physically destroy them or draw attention from local authorities, two reasons used to outlaw skateboarding from public spaces. Sedo interprets these travels as "an incipient imperialist imperative," through which the US is positioned as skateboarding's hegemony and other parts of the world as a periphery readily available for a skate-infused form of colonization and exploitation. These frontiers resound in the imaginations of these traveling skaters, expanding the hegemonic cartography and promising "discovery, challenge, and, ultimately, the capacity to find more spots, to keep the trail going" (McDuie-Ra 2021: 161). Skateboarding's craft, we hold, can reproduce colonial narratives of domination, territorialization, and orientalism.

Voyages with the aim of discovering and documenting "untouched" spots and "new skate scenes," while distributing such knowledge on hegemonic platforms, exist achingly close to the aims and ambitions of early travel writers, ethnographers, and missionaries. This is especially prevalent among skate travelers who believe that emancipatory and healing characteristics are intrinsic to boards and sideways movements – and must be experienced across the globe. Here, skateboarding can act as an unforeseen device for cultural assimilation and colonialist expansionism. In Seoul, for instance, there is a tension between skaters who film themselves against the backdrop of iconic Korean architecture and those who seek spots that mimic a Californian look and feel. What's at stake are conflicting ideals of what skateboarding *is*, and *for whom*: a decidedly American culture that needs to be emulated, or a practice that is necessarily localized and site-specific? The presence of American soldiers, some of whom skate during the evenings and weekends, and the travels by influential skaters are a pivot point for understanding these dynamics (Hölsgens 2021).

Such territorializing imperatives are decidedly gendered, privileging "the rights and freedom of men over those of women" (Abulhawa 2020: 74). As Dutch Olympian Candy Jacobs says on a Pushing Boarders (2019) panel,

> I was [sponsored by] Etnies for a year or ten. I was on flow and got a lot of shoes, which was sick. But all I wanted to do was get on a van and go on trips. I offered, 'hey, I'll pay you money, I wanna go on this trip, and I'll buy my own flight. Let me know where you are, I'll be there.' That opportunity never came up and I still have that need to fit in… I don't think it's just about fitting in, but also about being valued for the work I put in, all the hours that went into skateboarding and not getting that interview, not getting that photo.

This ethos of gate-keeping, then, is multifaceted. On the one hand, place-protective action is part of the reason why skate alternatives to TripAdvisor and Yelp hardly succeed: the whereabouts of spots are predominantly shared in person or via specialist photography and videography. Keeping this knowledge within a local skate community helps to limit the chance of spots being blown out, outlawed, or demolished. Gate-keeping can even be a means to push back against orientalist conceptions of skate spots – preventing the skateboarding's hegemonic industry from exploiting "untouched" spots (Hölsgens 2018). On the other hand, exclusionary governance may result in discriminatory practices, obstructing the accessibility of spots to divergent skate communities. These spots of desire hold variegated socio-political meanings, waltzing between local community formation, globalist colonization, and corporate strategies of exclusion.

Figure 3.2 Fidel and Lucas at the Big Four, MACBA Museum of Contemporary Art of Barcelona.

Source: Photo by Louisa Menke.

A curb eulogy

Skaters seek pleasure on the ruly and unruly edges of the Anthropocene. The fact that "almost 90 percent of passenger miles traveled in America are in cars and trucks" (McKibben 2023, online) is poignant bliss: its paved paradise (Grabar 2023) generates a grey, smooth, and standardized road ecology at once enticing to skaters and irrevocably destructive to our planet. Skaters – and their non-skating neighbors – are forced to live with and negotiate the toxins of the (post-)industrial-built environment: what counts as a skateable clime may also generate physical disease and social hostility. As a result, the communities tending toward curb-like spots are disproportionately affected and thus in negotiation with their polluting environs: brownfields, harbors, factory sites, bridges, plazas, and parking lots. And yet, skaters actively engage the grey spaces of the city as if they were their very source of life and happiness, showing care for their wellbeing, and endowing some with sacred meaning (O'Connor 2019). Waxing ledges and rails, fixing cracks with Bondo, and even pouring concrete in carefully prepared molds for DIY obstacles are part of the skater's toolkit (McDuie-Ra and Campbell 2023). Recent anecdotal evidence shows that some skaters even talk to their spots of desire, both figuratively and literally, endowing them with a totem and idol subjectivity: a craft fetishism.

Still, the meanings skaters attribute to spots are as variegated as our biodiverse environments once were. Consider the premise of *Urban Pamphleteer: Skateboardings*, a print publication one of us was involved in:

> The lived experiences of skateboarders of colour, of diverse genders and sexualities, of different mobilities and class backgrounds, intersect with the politics of their everyday lives and negotiations with public and private space. With this in mind, we ask: what does a skateable space look and feel like, and for whom?
>
> (Callan-Riley and Hölsgens 2020: i)

Following the tradition of radical pamphleteering, the issue positions curbs as a spatial typology eliciting the hopes, desires, and worries of the global skate community. What appears to be meaningless to the uninformed eye is a "eulogized space" for others (Bachelard 2014: 19): a curb is an urban feature as loved by skaters as it is ignored by the public. The pamphlet's cover is a close-up shot of a damaged curb: granular and crusty. The curb has seen some life – a skater's life, most likely. The remnants of wax, grinds, and slides are still arrestingly present. It's a detailed image, showing the weeds on the side of the road, the rocky structure of asphalt, and the smooth concrete tiles of pavement. There's hardly any depth to the image, making it difficult to denote which elements are vertically raised. An unnoticing glance offers only a flat surface separated by a range of grey materials. But a skater's body always notices, identifies, imagines. A microhabitat of sorts, the curb is a counterpoint to the Blubba, the architectural cornerstone creatively reimagined by Anthony Pappalardo. Though less injurious and contentious, a curb is unobtrusive and mundane. Still, within the context of the pamphleteer, it stands in for memories, controlled fear, a sense of belonging, nomadism, and inclusion. To skate a curb is to craft the city.

For her contribution to the pamphleteer, performance researcher Dani Abulhawa (2020) takes cues from the built environment to realize dance improvisations. This includes "lumps in the concrete; open flat areas; painted lines, words ('exit') and arrows; the curvature of walls; hidden areas and curbs" (Abulhawa 2020: 15). Everyday architecture is reappropriated for play and performance, transforming hidden parking spots and neglected road crossings into a stadium for creativity and, typically, pro-social good. Abulhawa skates in a car park, "creating the smallest and slowest movements" she could perform (idem: 15) – to the point of laying down on the flat surface, her board within an arm's reach. Occupying a car park – a nonplace – without an engine-driven vehicle is a prefiguration: *imagine the things we could do if there were fewer cars?* An emptied car park, with its well-maintained curbs and curling-smooth tarmac, offers a spatial framework for rethinking what a skate-friendly city might look like. What's more, the skateboard as tool cultivates a feeling of safety through an aesthetic of masculinity. As Abulhawa (idem: 13) writes, "As a teenager, I would put my hood up and walk home at night with my skateboard, adopting a kind of invisibility cloud, or more accurately, a masculine one." The skate-infused dance improvisation builds upon such sensibilities, exploring what makes a space friendly to and safe for skaters. The curb and skateboard symbolize such safety, offering a temporary refuge from gender discrimination.

But not all skateable spaces are inviting to all. In his contribution on queer skate organizations, skate critic Tobias Coughlin-Bogue (2020) explores the relationality between assemblages of skate spots and inclusivity. Crowded skateparks tend to be structured around clans of "cisgender straight men, and few of them are willing to jeopardize their membership to help non-traditional skaters feel welcome" (idem: 20). Smaller spots dispersed across town – like curbs – secure private and safer environs for learning tricks and building community. This, the "straight-presenting queer skater" (idem: 18) intimates, is why LGBTQ+ collective *Unity* meets up at a single curb at the parking lot of a tram station, seeking a socio-spatial alternative to heteronormative and male-dominated skateparks. Like Abulhawa's car park, *Unity*'s curb is a pivot point for understanding what makes a spot desirable. Here, too, the prerequisite of skateability is the absence of hostility: at times, adversity emerges *from within*, resulting in an inclination toward decentralized urban space. To this point, Coughlin-Bogue (2020: 18–19) notes that the curb is a skater's totem, a layer in its dispersed sediment that equalizes as much as it energizes:

> We need to bring back the days of itinerant street skating. By doing this, not only will we provide more space for people who have been disenfranchised by skateboarding to practice in private, which is more crucial in a subculture where skills equals social capital, but we will also more quickly achieve an integrated skate culture.

Scattered curbs inform a skater's arrhythmic and nomadic knowledge of the city. Curbs encourage practitioners to travel between spots – contributing to psychogeographic knowledge of the city and health benefits from transit on foot, board, or bike. Key, here, is both a socially welcoming environment and the accessibility of the street. As Felipe Nunes states later on in the same issue: "My biggest challenge when I'm skating on the streets and in different cities is when the street has no pavement [...] Ramps can definitely make access easier to everybody and cities would be much better for getting around" (Rubin and Nunes 2020: 25). A seated skater, Nunes sees a connection between the skateability of spots and the broader accessibility of public space. A curb cut and tactile paving, features of the urban Universal Design revolution, are as much a tool for daily mobility as a skateable obstacle. Stronger yet, America's "first curbs cuts, designed for wheelchair users, were installed just as sidewalk surfing was taking off. It was this push to facilitate rolling travel in the downtown areas that would create the ecosystem for skateboarding" (idem: 23).

Historicizing spots

Unlike the conceptualization of place, a skate spot denotes something unmistakably ephemeral and transient. As it usually lacks any formal recognition, let alone a heritage status, it is as easily demolished as it is identified – often in the shadows of gentrification strategies. And yet, regardless of such an uncertain lifespan, spots are socially adopted by a community of practitioners. This includes an ethic of care, from pulling weeds and sweeping dirt to fixing cracks and building DIY modifications (McDuie-Ra and Campbell 2023). This "clandestine upkeep" instills "a communal practice that entails discretion and fine-tuning" (Vivoni and Folsom-Fraster 2021: 313). These crafts-like acts of solidarity and care have a secretive sway, as they mostly exist in a context of hostility: maintenance is a marker of ownership and could, and in some occasions should, be confused for squatting.

A recent exception to the paradoxical bind of impermanence and care is Civic Leeds, a grassroots initiative mobilized to cultivate inclusive and accessible skate spots. Their database maps not only the location of a spot but also its socio-material status and a set of situated etiquettes – an exception in skateboarding's acts of gate-keeping. Take a set of stairs and curbs at the Millennium Square, a spot amicably called "Civic." The database's curators suggest that late afternoons and weekends work best for skating, outside of the temporal parameters of work and commerce. But skating this spot comes with a responsibility: "Occasionally people will be getting married at the building so be nice, chip and come back later rather than getting [in] the way of someone's wedding photos" (Civic Leeds 2022). Cultivating social norms coincides with a push for skate-friendly policies, showing how the skate community can be a good partner to the city. In part, this is established through the curators' "established relationships with many of the institutions in Leeds that are commonly skated" (Civic Leeds 2022).

By making the database freely available and negotiating the skateability of spots with a range of urban stakeholders, Civic Leeds also draws attention to the civic responsibility skaters have. Instead of normalizing littering, public urination, or the illegal use of public space, the database includes information about public restrooms and grocery stores, while highlighting how to enjoy a spot without disturbing its non-skating users. This is perhaps best exemplified by the Henry Moore Institute, a center dedicated to the study, preservation, and exhibition of sculptures. At the entrance of the center is a set of stairs, accompanied by granite ledges particularly appealing to novice skaters. Despite attempts to regulate skateboarding, there was limited supervision during nighttime hours. For years, the spot was skated outside of office hours, resulting in cracks and fractures to the ledges. Enveloped in the Civic Leeds initiative, artist-researcher and skater Harry Meadley proposed turning one of the ledges into a durable, skateable sculpture. The agreement was that skaters would take care of the new ledges, while leaving the others intact.

The sculpture, *For SB*, has the shape of a regular ledge, the main difference being that the materials used are more resilient to trick play and easier to maintain and replace in case of superficial damage. Celebrating its launch on 16 and 17 September 2023, the sculpture now protects the architectural heritage of the Institute's outer plaza, as much as it is an acknowledged skate spot. Or, as the Henry Moore Institute (2023, online) communicates through its official channels,

> The work, titled For SB, sees an almost unnoticeable act of restoration take place to what is known by skateboarders as the 'Henry Moore ledge'. The restoration will help preserve its long-term use for the act of skateboarding, as well as limiting damage to the Grade 2 listed building elsewhere. We hope this mutually beneficial gesture sets an example for how street skating can become more embraced by arts institutions, which frequently find themselves being popular skate spots. The [launch] event highlights the Institute's importance as a site of cultural significance for a commonly misunderstood community, and our commitment to the skateboard community literally on our doorstep.

In short, skaters use spots like Civic and For SB as their arena, stadium, court, or workshop to perform their craft. Occasionally acquiring the status of sacralized sites of pilgrimage, acclaimed skate spots form social layers of sense-making, accumulated over time and pressure like sedimentary rock (O'Connor 2019). More recently, the city of Malmö recently purchased the ruins of Philadelphia's LOVE Park, transporting its stairs, ledges, and rails, in order to rebuild the plaza in Sweden. An iconic landmark to skaters, LOVE is an example of alternative considerations for cultural heritage. In Malmö, the purchased city features will act as a facsimile of the original, similar to how the town of Tianducheng in Hangzhou mimics Parisian architecture – including the Eiffel Tower, Champs-Élysées, and the Jardin du Luxembourg. The main difference: whereas Tianducheng's landmarks are replicas at best, LOVE Park in Malmö is built with the original materials. In so doing, this project pushes a decidedly international narrative of preservation and heritage, similar to how museums and galleries treat artworks. If anything, the transmutation of LOVE Park, as well as the institutional recognition of skateable sculpture For SB, suggests that skateboarding is, slowly but surely, moving from a countercultural ideology to a crafts-like sociality.

Note

1 Personal correspondence with authors.

References

Abulhawa, D. (2020). *Skateboarding and Femininity: Gender, Space-Making and Expressive Movement*. London: Routledge.

Bachelard, G. (2014). *The Poetics of Space*. London: Penguin.

Beal, B., & Ebeling, K.. (2019). "Can You Sell Out if You've Never Been in? The Olympics and Creating Spaces for Gender Inclusion in Skateboarding." In Schwier, J., & Kilberth, V. (eds.). *Skateboarding between Subculture and Olympics*, 97–116. Bielefeld: Transcript.

Boas, F. (1927[1955]). *Primitive Art*. New York: Dover.

Borden, I. (2001). *Skateboarding, Space and the City: Architecture and the Body*. Oxford: Berg Publishers.

Callan-Riley, T., & Hölsgens, S. (2020). *Urban Pamphleteer# 8 Skateboardings*. London: Urban Laboratory.

Chamarette, J. (2012). *Phenomenology and the Future of Film*. Hampshire: Palgrave Macmillan.

Cianciotto, L. M. (2020). "Public Space, Common Space, and the Spaces In–Between: A Case Study of Philadelphia's Love Park." *City & Community*, 19.3: 676–703.

Civic Leeds. (2022). "Spot Guides," https://www.civicleeds.com/spots/.

Coughlin-Bogue, T. (2020). *Queering Skateble Space. Urban Pamphleteer #8 Skateboardings*, 18–20. Hölsgens, S., & Callan-Riley, T. (eds.). London: UCL Urban Lab.

Deleuze, G., & Guattari, F. (1987). *A Thousand Plateaus: Capitalism and Schizophrenia*. London: Athlone Press.

Dickinson, S., Millie, A., & Peters, E. (2022). "Street Skateboarding and the Aesthetic Order of Public Spaces." *The British Journal of Criminology*, 62.6: 1454–1469.

D'Orazio, D. (2020). "The Skate Video Revolution: How Promotional Film Changed Skateboarding Subculture." *The International Journal of Sport and Society*, 11.3: 55–72.

Glenney, B. (2023). "Polluted Leisure Enskilment: Skateboarding as Ecosophy." *Leisure Sciences*, 2023: 1–25.

Golding, F. (2024). "Five Favorite Parts With Ben Kadow." *Quartersnacks*, 7 February 2024, https://quartersnacks.com/2024/02/five-favorite-parts-with-ben-kadow/.

Gowlland, G. (2015). "Unpacking Craft Skills: What Can Images Reveal about the Embodied Experience of Craft?" *Visual Anthropology*, 28.4: 286–297.

Grabar, H. (2023). *Paved Paradise: How Parking Explains the World*. New York: Penguin Press.

Henry Moore Institute (2023). *Civic Skateboarding at the Henry Moore Institute*, 12 September 2023, https://henry-moore.org/civic-skateboarding-at-the-henry-moore-institute/.

Hölsgens, S. (2018). *A Phenomenology of Skateboarding in Seoul, South Korea: Experiential and Filmic Observations*. UCL: PhD Thesis.

Hölsgens, S. (2021). *Skateboarding in Seoul: A Sensory Ethnography*. Groningen: University of Groningen Press.

Hölsgens, S. (2024). "Learning to See or How to Make Sense of the Skillful Things Skateboarders Do." In Vannini, P. (ed.). *The Routledge International Handbook of Sensory Ethnography*, 387–400. New York: Routledge.

Ingold, T. (2000). *The Perception of the Environment: Essays on Livelihood, Dwelling and Skill*. London: Taylor & Francis Group.

Ingold, T. (2004). "Culture on the Ground." *Journal of Material Culture*, 9.3: 315–340.

Kale, S. (2016). "Visions of Los Angeles: Landscape Architect Lawrence Halprin Transforms the City." *The Halprin Workshops, 1966-1971*, https://experiments.californiahistoricalsociety.org/visions-of-los-angeles/.

Latour, B. (2005). *Re-Assembling the Social*. Oxford: Oxford University Press.

Lelchuk, I. (2003). "U.N. Plaza's architect to fight redesign/Famed planner calls S.F. plan no answer to drunks, homeless." *San Francisco Chronicle*, 18 April 2003,

https://www.sfgate.com/bayarea/article/u-n-plaza-s-architect-to-fight-redesign-famed-2654628.php.
Malinowski, B. (1922[2014]). *Argonauts of the Western Pacific.* London: Routledge.
Marks, L. (2000). *The Skin of the Film: Intercultural Cinema, Embodiment, and the Senses.* Durham: Duke University Press.
Martin, T. (2021). *Craft Learning as Perceptual Transformation.* Berlin: Springer.
McDuie-Ra, D. (2021). *Skateboarding and Urban Landscapes in Asia: Endless Spots.* Amsterdam: Amsterdam University Press.
McDuie-Ra, D., & Campbell, J. (2023). "Preparing Surfaces for Shredding: Skateboarding, Repair, and Care across Scales." *Area*, 55.4: 496–505.
McKibben, B. (2023). "Toward a Land of Buses and Bikes". *The New York Review* 5 October 2023 issue, https://www.nybooks.com/articles/2023/10/05/toward-a-land-of-buses-and-bikes-crossings-ben-goldfarb/.
O'Connor, P. (2019). *Skateboarding and Religion.* Berlin: Springer Nature.
Pushing Boarders (2019). *The Revolution Will Not Be Patronised*, https://www.youtube.com/watch?v=cBhwjS8dw-k.
Rendell, J. (2007). "Site-Writing: She Is Walking about in a Town Which She Does Not Know." *Home Cultures*, 4.2: 177–199.
Roberts, C. (2021). *The Nine Club. Anthony Claravall. Episode 191*, https://www.youtube.com/watch?v=sFl02BdNFHw.
Rubin, B., Nunes, F. (2020). *Skateboarding and Mobility. Urban Pamphleteer #8 Skateboardings*, 23–25. Hölsgens, S. & Callan-Riley, T. (eds.). London: UCL Urban Lab.
Sedo, T. (2010). "Dead-Stock Boards, Blown-Out Spots, and the Olympic Games: Global Twists and Local Turns in the Formation of China's Skateboarding Community". In Rethmann, P., Szeman, I., & Coleman, W. (eds.). *Cultural Autonomy: Frictions and Connections*, 257–290. Vancouver: UBC Press.
Sennett, R. (2008). *The Craftsman.* New Haven: Yale University Press.
Sobchack, V. (1992). *The Address of the Eye: A Phenomenology of Film Experience.* Princeton: Princeton University Press.
Soltz, W. (2016). "Lawrence Halprin and Two Modern Spaces." In Breyfogle, N., Conn, S., & Offenburger, A. (eds.). *Origins: Current Events in Historical Perspective.* The Ohio State University and Miami University.
Toeda, Y. (2024). *Nanaka Fujisawa/Hand rail battle*, https://www.youtube.com/watch?v=6bAbCCWMgs0&t=1s, last accessed 4 March 2024.
Vivoni, F., & Folsom-Fraster, J. (2021). "Crafting Cities for All: Qualitative Inquiry of the Street and the Spatial Practice of Skateboarding." *Cultural Studies ↔ Critical Methodologies*, 21.4: 311–318.
Watson, M., & Shove, E. (2008). "Product, Competence, Project and Practice: DIY and the Dynamics of Craft Consumption." *Journal of Consumer Culture*, 8.1: 69–89.
Woolley, H., & Johns, R. (2001). "Skateboarding: The City as a Playground." *Journal of Urban Design*, 6.2: 211–230.

4 Failure and the Senses
A Skate Pedagogy of Care and Resilience

Learning to skate equates to bruises, scratches, skin traumas, and twisted ankles. Bodily agony is part of the magical bind of skateboarding, of its sensory history. As skate critic Kyle Beachy (2021: 12) writes, "If you want to know skateboarding […] look at a skater's elbows. Examine their shins." But repeated failure can take a heavy toll: a skater's aging body tends to be busted and fractured, damaged by years of hard-fought tricks play. Should we restrict skateboarding to supervised skateparks and enforce protective gear to break the cycle of pain and suffering, as medical reports and parks departments suggest? Or are slam trophies that champion the skater who endures, who falls and gets back up, who skates to the bitter end?

This chapter addresses how failure is imagined and represented in skate culture today. We start by introducing how failure deepens our understanding of the complex ecology of skate culture – its spots and spaces, its sensory models, and its community formation. We then consider how certain skaters show us why it may be better if we all started to skate a tad slower and speculate a type of skating that is, conceivably, less harmful. In particular, we unpack a slogan introduced by nonprofit *Skate Like a Girl* (SLAG): "skate slow and live." This slogan offers a hopeful and empowering example of skateboarding as a pedagogical tool for positive social change, where scabbed knees and crusted elbows stand in for collective empowerment.

This is skateboarding

What's a failure for some is a success for others. This is intriguingly present in skate media of past and current times. From renowned magazines like *Thrasher* (1981–) and *Big Brother* (1992–2004) to videos such as Zero's *Thrill of It All* (1997) and Emerica's *This is Skateboarding* (2003), the capture of skill progression has been at the heart of the representation of skate culture for over four decades. "And how *fun* they are to watch," writes Kyle Beachy (2021: 11), "how visceral at times, like little grenades of spectacles that explode with affect." Ideologically, these affective and emotive explosions confound in a tendency to celebrate the failure of the tumbling skater (Hölsgens and O'Connor

DOI: 10.4324/9781003510642-4
This chapter has been made available under a CC-BY-NC-ND 4.0 license.

2022). Take the opening sequence of Heath Kirchart's video part in *This is Skateboarding*. The part exploits all main features of the modern skate video: it is spectacle-driven, amplifies an underground aesthetic, and centers around male athletes who perform at their very best. The video opens with a fight of sorts: a business man in a tie yells at a filmer, "Get the fuck out of that tree!" and turns his attention to Kirchart, "Get out of here!" Into his phone he pleads, "We've got a bunch of skateboarders here and they're hostile." Kirchart seems unimpressed, "*We* are getting hostile?" he says as he decides to leave – respecting the man's demand to stop skating. The opening sequence symbolically positions the skater as an unwanted figure, an outcast, an intruder.

The scenes that follow change everything. We see Kirchart skate on the greyest of concrete, at night. A filmer follows him at close distance, riding a skateboard himself and using a fisheye-lens on a Sony VX1000 and an all-too-flashy LED light to capture the spectacle of tricks. Kirchart lands a tailslide and fakie flip, two fairly basic though perfectly executed tricks, after which he noticeably prepares himself for something more impressive, more masculine. He accelerates and heads into darkness in the unknown distance. Then, we – as spectators – see a massive set of stairs emerge in front of him, lit with another filmer in the waiting. Without hesitation or despair, Kirchart ollies onto the top of the ledge on the left-hand side of the stairs. He grinds for a few inches, before his front truck clips on an irregularity of an otherwise smooth surface. He trips, about twelve feet above ground level, head over heel into a grey abyss. We feel his body splat. We see a second angle and the fall feels endless; the height of the stair set appears to be beyond human scale. The closer Kirchart gets to the immutable asphalt, the more horizontal his body.

Any informed spectator knows: this will not end well. And it doesn't. Kirchart falls flat on his chest and face. The impact of the fall is painstakingly audible because of the industrious recording by semi-professional audiovisual equipment. The fall punctuates the video's opening sequence. The social hostility of the business man is matched by the material hostility of the grey pavement below the stair set. In the backdrop, we see a videographer. He does not move, as if aloof from the fall (or numbed by all the falls he's seen over the course of his professional careers). We don't get to see whether Kirchart is doing well, nor do we ever find out whether the videographer moves over to help him. As passive spectators, we only get the bail. What follows are black-and-white-images of Kirchart smoking, manifesting his nebulous and legendary status, concluded by a daytime sequence of him successfully landing the trick. There is no other trace of the failed attempt, materially or discursively.

Learning to play

This, Heath Kirchart's video part suggests, *is skateboarding*. In reckless abandon, skaters fall and slam, hurt themselves, and sometimes (eventually) succeed. Pedagogically, this kind of narrative makes a whole lot of sense. Skaters, through repeated failure, incrementally master the kinds of tricks previously beyond their skill level. But Kirchart is not your everyday professional skater. He is risk-seeking as well, embarking on "death-defying travel missions," including riding a raft through the grand canyon, cross-country cycling, free climbing in Yosemite, and sailing from San Diego to Todos Santos (Vice 2022). Phenomenologically, Kirchart engages in existential risk, foregrounding a sensory potentiality of failure. His skating is also about testing the limits of the human body, seeking pleasure in risk-centered activities.

Philosopher Hubert Dreyfus (1991) analyzes this kind of praxis through phenomenology of skill acquisition: through repetition and practice, Dreyfus claims, a novice not only learns the rules of a game or activity but also trains the capacity to respond to unknown situations. An expert no longer actively enacts trained routines and regulations but rather seems to constantly improvise: they can respond to the unique circumstances of a particular moment, intuitively knowing how best to act. Simply put: they have sufficient *experience* and *knowledge* to rely on and can usually act quickly, seemingly effortlessly or even thoughtlessly. As an expert, they replace ritualistic performance of rules for enskiled flexibility performed on the fly.

This typology of enskilment applies to many bodily practices. Car drivers first learn by practicing rules and regulations and, second, becoming attuned to the car as an extension of their body. Eventually, and thanks to their trained expertise, they simply *do*, attuning themselves to the specificities of a context. Similarly, Dreyfus (1991) says, an expert chess player no longer has to calculate the best move: they simply *see* what would be most useful or strategic in a particular movement, and act accordingly. Once rules and regulations are made familiar and become part of one's embodied practices, (informed and trained) intuition can take over. In this learning process, skills and techniques become a subjective signature – individualized through the specificities of one's learning conditions, surroundings, and somatics (Chapter 2).

One of the main differences between an activity like car driving and most sports is the role of failure. Driving instructors – we hope – prevent their students from crashing into other vehicles, whereas tennis coaches encourage their trainees to take risks during training sessions. Precisely by over-shooting or hitting the net, tennis players learn to gauge the limits of the court and master the game. In play, risks-taking is the crux to mastery. Pushing against rule-binding parameters leads to tacit knowledge as to how to stay (just) within rules. Unlike driving a car as a mode of transportation, the point of playing tennis is not to play it safely. Rather, a shot landing on the outer lines of the court is generally difficult to reach for opponents. Risk shots may increase the chances of winning a point – when hit successfully.

Learning to skate correlates to such risk-taking as well. Like tennis, there is an element of play to the praxis of skating: it's fun, free, distinct from ordinary life, and done for the sake of it (Huizinga 2008). Yet, failure in skateboarding

Failure and the Senses 49

Figure 4.1 Alina skating downhill from the Montjuïc hill in Barcelona.
Source: Photo by Louisa Menke.

results in more than a missed shot, being offside, or the offshoot injury. There are no referees or rules overseeing and protecting players from unhealthy behavior. Instead, skaters have historically correlated failure with pain rather than penalty, normalizing injurious practices of play and spectacle. For this reason, it's quite telling that a trick successfully landed after repeated failure is called a "make" (Dixon 2011). What's painstakingly present is the frequency of the painful fall, adding a felt embodied dimension to its athletic practice. Success for a skater is thus more than playing within the boundaries of protective rules and regulations. Rather, it is the repetitive process of painstakingly trying to land a trick.

Failure and redemption

A make is a sacred destination rarely reached. With each attempt, this goal is being ritualized in pain, made in resilience. Skaters settle on a trick as if it's their calling. Before going to the streets, a trick is often visualized, studied, dreamt, or imagined. Attempts to land a trick can last days, months, or even years. These efforts are shared, too: skaters know which tricks peers are working up to. As such, skill acquisition takes on more than a physiological and psychological meaning. It has a sociological upshot, as the hoped-for outcome exceeds the sports-like goal of playing within the rules of the game: tricks, here, are more like a performative signature move than a rule-driven drill. The resolution – a make – is spiritual redemption rather than a competitive edge. Filmers often zoom in on the face of the skater after a make, allowing the viewer to witness the exhalation of success.

Skateboarding is a pedagogy of resolve, only knowable to those who remember the feeling of scabbed and swollen elbows and crusted knees. When performing a trick, the skater's body is in the air, floating above and rarely touching the skateboard, desiring a clean and aesthetically pleasing landing. Like Sisyphus, skaters know that this desire for success is futile (Buckareff 2021). The joy of each and every landed trick never lasts: it aspires to renew itself, by way of a new consecrated destination and a similar rite of passage: skaters simply move on to a new trick, another decorum, and start all over. The "make" is short-lived, a temporary resolve: it is but a step toward the next mountain. As Jose Vadi (2022, online) writes, "When landing a trick after hours of trying, you feel not so much a celebration but an exhalation, a release of relief." Akin to joint cracking, a make is a popping sensation of satisfaction and felicity. Such a relief makes up for all the sweat, dehydration, stench, and skin-deep wounds that co-occur with a skater's skill acquisition – temporarily.

These religious and mythological associations, a "pilgrim's progress," hold a generative meaning. Sociologist Paul O'Connor (2019) considers how religion acts as a generative framework for understanding skate culture. In particular, he suggests that skateboarding is awash with spirituality, from the ritual of learning a new trick to an economy of gift exchange. What's important, here, is that play – within skateboarding – is an unstable state, located somewhere between lifestyle sports and spiritual immersion, between pain and pleasure, between restriction and freedom. This instability can be temporarily resolved through a make, which "stabilizes and grounds skaterly identity" (Dixon 2011, online). Somatically, skaters are their latest trick, similar to how a religious identity is confirmed and re-established during each prayer of contrition, each visit to its temple, and each pilgrimage to its Walhalla. Failure, in this reading, becomes a hurdle to overcome, at whatever cost. It points to one's signature as a skater, similar to how stance denotes one's orientation within and toward the world (Chapter 2).

This even applies to competitive skateboarding. Here, too, skaters rarely string together well-scoring tricks without any consideration for personal feats, aesthetic pleasure, or symbolic meaning. Consider the final few minutes of the 2023 Street League Super Crown in São Paulo, regularly regarded as the world championship for skateboarding. Aoi Uemura – one of the most promising talents of her generation – is ranked sixth, a dozen points behind leading skater Rayssa Leal. No matter the outcome of her final trick attempt, a gold medal is out of reach. What's more, the previous two attempts resulted in slams, bracketing an otherwise "successful" performance.

Despite or precisely because of this competitive failure, Uemura shows nothing but joy in the lead-up to her final attempt. She smiles, energetically waving her hands at the audience to get them excited. The commentators are acutely aware of the stakes: "Aoi is in sixth place. She can't win, but she could go out in a blaze of glory" (SLS 2024). Riding up to the handrail, she looks focused yet relaxed. A kicker elevates her body, as if suspended in air, before she starts sliding on the yellow railing. After a perfectly executed slide, Uemura sticks the landing: a make. Within a split-second, she cheers as if she's won the championship – her make *is* a win. The landed lipslide reaffirms her skater's identity: rather than gold, what's won is *personal glory*. What's more, she is a different person than she was before. It's a sacred moment, ritualistically overcoming the failure of previous attempts, as much as it's an athletic achievement of a non-white athlete in a competitive context (Williams 2022).

Arguably, the Olympic Games and competitions like Street League are a pivot point – recentering skateboarding as a sport by foregrounding high-scoring tricks, prize money, statistics, and mainstream acclaim. To a certain extent, the make echoes performances of non-skating athletes who cherish a personal best over medals. Uemura draws attention to what she considers worth cheering for: the poetics of a landed trick after repeated efforts. Yet here's the complication: Uemura does so in the context of the world championship, sponsored by Cup Noodles, Chevrolet, and Tiger Beer, in a time and age where women skaters struggle to make a living without the support of such brands (Beal and Ebeling 2019). Competitive edge, here, correlates to professional opportunity. Oscillating between the marketplace and poetics, between arts and sports, Uemura's trick performance holds a range of potentially contradictory meanings. The narrative of failure and success, here, corresponds to both a neoliberal achievement and ritualistic, even spiritual pleasure. When play and work are collapsed, as is the case in the Street League world championships, a hydra emerges – a many-headed, enchanting activity at once fun and competitive. How, then, do we make sense of success and failure in skateboarding? What do these concepts signify to skaters and their spectators? It's to these questions that we now turn.

A gnarly epistemology

"Sensing," writes anthropologist Anna Harris (2020: 16), "is a process, shaped by a mutual interplay between individuals and others, materials, words and the worlds inhabited." Alongside developing their stance, skaters learn to sense through failure, interfaced by the skateboard as their tool and urban space as their decorum. The repeated act of falling intimates a sensory attunement to the built environment: experienced skaters *know* the tacit difference between wooden and granite surfaces. They recall the feeling of traversing humid or freezing cold environments not only because of their skateability but also because of their potentiality to hurt the human body. This felt immediacy of scratches, abrasions, punctures, and avulsions locates the skater's knowledge on a skin-deep level: *the body remembers*. The sensory engagement with the city, a bruising and radiating matter, is acutely felt (Hölsgens

2018a). Urban space inflicts a hurting, perhaps even vicious, affect on skaters, who, in turn, learn through looped failure. This dialectic of pleasure and pain offers a poignant counterpoint to the kind of activities regularly praised for meditative, healthy, and therapeutic characteristics – such as walking, knitting, gardening, fishing, dancing, and cooking.

This dialectic holds socio-somatic meaning. Skaters have the capacity to instantaneously discern whether urban space is not only skateable but also *gnarly* – meaning: dangerous, exciting, provocative, risky, and thus full of untapped pleasure. Paraphrasing sociologist Kevin Low (2015), skateboarding "comes with a sense of duality," being both full of pleasure and grit, merging health and destruction, and adversity and care. Socially, then, failure can act as an interface for ordering authenticity, separating "core skaters" from "mainstream consumers" (Dupont 2014). Like wearing helmets or other protective gear, taking lessons on how to skate (including how to fall) has historically coincided with stigmatization: wearing helmets or taking lessons remains contested among hardcore skaters, including Olympic athletes (cf. Corwin et al. 2019; Robinson 2021). But this alleged hierarchy between core and mainstream neglects who *can* and *cannot* afford to skate at gnarly spots. A school teacher may not be able to risk hurting their wrists, knowing that the shortage of educators means they cannot be easily replaced in case of an injury. A well-established distinction between work and nonwork is not tenable for all, as most lives are punctuated by a capitalist ideology of productivity and professionalism. This even applies to professional skaters: during our fieldwork we noted that Olympic hopefuls – especially those living in precarity – reduced the time spent at gnarly spots.

By contrast, failure, injuries, and gnarly spots can hold socio-economic meaning, too. The harder or more brutal the fall, the tastier future victory and success, suggesting one cannot exist without the other: "when falling becomes an option, however controllable, scabs on elbows like encrusted merit badges, earned by trying to learn something new" (Vadi 2022, online). The archetypical skate video – focusing on street skating and the spectacle of tricks – is 1) a marketing tool to sell products and 2) celebrates failure as a cornerstone to success. A bail is as pleasurable as a landed trick: both accredit and mythologize the professional skater, whose attire and hardware are showcased for purchase. The role of failure is not to be underestimated in this marketing strategy: the higher the stair set, bigger the obstacle, or longer the handrail, the more laudable the skater's fall and/or make. This is most vividly seen in Heath Kirchart's video part in *This Is Skateboarding*. Failure has become part of Kirchart's trademark and legacy, as he confirms in an interview video by *The Berrics* (2018): "When people message me, they definitely only talk about the slams. Like, people seem to care a lot more about all that than anything you've ever made." The interviewer responds: "I always say, sometimes a slam is just as good as a make." Kirchart: "It's better. You get way more longevity out of it. I mean, look, you're not sitting here talking to me about whatever I *made*, right?"

Amplifying Kirchart's comment, a skater is immortalized because of their slams. Commercially, there's value to failure – as long as your livelihood doesn't rely on prize money from competitions. Symbolically, the skateable obstacle is an object of desire and a signifier of pleasure, perhaps even a locale for worship. What makes this neoliberal is a mutual bond between a "drive for self-improvement" (Howes 2023: 43) and the far-reaching commodification and commercialization of sensory modalities. Put differently, failure in skateboarding is historically constructed, communicating socio-economic values by attending to cultural imaginaries. The multifaceted praxis of seeking success through failure is perfectly captured in two mantras with origins in the 1980s: "Skate or Die" and "Skate and Destroy." Both point toward the dominant narrative of self-reliance and neoliberal achievement, as much as they are commodities in and of themselves. Coined and branded by *Thrasher Magazine*, "Skate and Destroy" is about finding and dominating skateable space in the built environment. Destruction, here, is positioned as a claim to fame, as it showcases a skater's capacity to own a spot by leaving an irreversible mark on it. Made popular by the titular video game from 1987, Skate or Die refers to an individual's commitment to skateboarding: being a skater is a lifestyle precisely by being a manifestation of freedom.

Giving up on one's identity as a skater is no option: *one rather dies than stops skating*. Geographically, this technique runs parallel to the fetishization of skateable space: traveling to sites unvisited, hoping to find *new* spots to dominate. As Seoul-based skate writer Martyn Conrad (Kim 2013: 44, also see Hölsgens 2021) writes,

> there is a certain kind of feeling that washes over you when you successfully seek out and skate a new spot. It's something about the creativity of transforming mundane objects into something more exotic (...) We [skaters] habitually examine the subtle nuances of the slopes and textures of everything we see. Like an invasive species, we can adapt to any environment.

Gazed at with a skater's eye, any obstacle will be territorialized, socially deconstructing its banal meaning for the beautiful. No matter the cost.

"Skate slow and live"

SLAG is a nonprofit organization set up to empower women, non-binary and trans people. Formed in 2000 in Seattle, SLAG runs skate lessons, diversity workshops, and summer camps with the aim to create "an inclusive community by promoting confidence, leadership, and social justice through skateboarding" (Skate Like a Girl online). Over the past five years, SLAG generated mainstream attention, not least because of an increased interest within and beyond the sports industry in diversity, equity, and inclusion policies (Abulhawa 2020; Willing and Pappalardo 2023). More recently, the nonprofit partnered up with brands like Nike and Spitfire, working toward a collection of apparel distributed globally across skate and sports retail. As SLAG's executive director Kristin Ebeling says about the Nike partnership: "We're really challenging who and how people skateboard. All the things that we think about our skate culture, we're like, 'Hmm, does that have to be skate culture? Does that have to be everyone's skate culture?' (...) The process also gave us an opportunity to elevate community members as well as youth" (Nike 2022, online). Reappropriating the marketplace for affirmative action is considered a way to effect positive change in a male-dominated industry, to work toward intentionally inclusive skate and sports brands. SLAG exemplifies how two decades of prefigurative politics can result in new socialities, corporate strategies, and media representation – symbolized by Wimbledon winner Carlos Alcaraz wearing a SLAG-branded Nike shirt in the Netflix tennis documentary "Break Point" (Webb 2024).

In 2022, Nike Skateboarding and SLAG co-released *Transenders* (Cheng 2022), a ten-minute film "exploring how the power of community allows you to be your true self, overcome failure, and transcend fear." Not unlike Emerica's *This is Skateboarding*, the film includes extended sequences solely focusing on trick play, but this is by no means a hegemonic skate video: instead of video parts tailored to individuals, the narrative structures around community building and identity formation. *Transenders* opens with a series of contrasts: dark/light, failure/success, and ephemerality/eternity. We hear a voice-over: "Those moments of joy in skateboarding are so fleeting. You can spend all day practicing a trick. And every attempt you make you just fall." The image turns from a night scene to a skatepark at midday. A skater drops in, preparing for a trick. We hear something unusual, something sports-like, something *kind*: a bunch of people cheer the skater on, chanting her name – "Alexa, Alexa, Alexa, Alexa!" The voice-over continues: "And there might be this one moment where you land the ollie or you're successful at whatever you're trying to do. And it's those seconds that change everything. You never forget those moments."

Throughout *Transenders*, we see skaters walk, hang out, and skate together – denouncing the idea that skateboarding is an individual, destructive, spectacle-driven practice. What's at stake is a prefiguration of what skateboarding *could* be: cooperative instead of egocentric, caring instead of destructive, communal rather than solo, and welcoming instead of gatekeeping. This position becomes especially evident when Alexa touches upon the notion of failure: "I think the moments of fear are really propelled by the community around you. The consequence of falling or failing won't stop you from being a skateboarder. What stops you are people at the skatepark who bully you out of it." Failure, here, is *queer failure*, being more than a

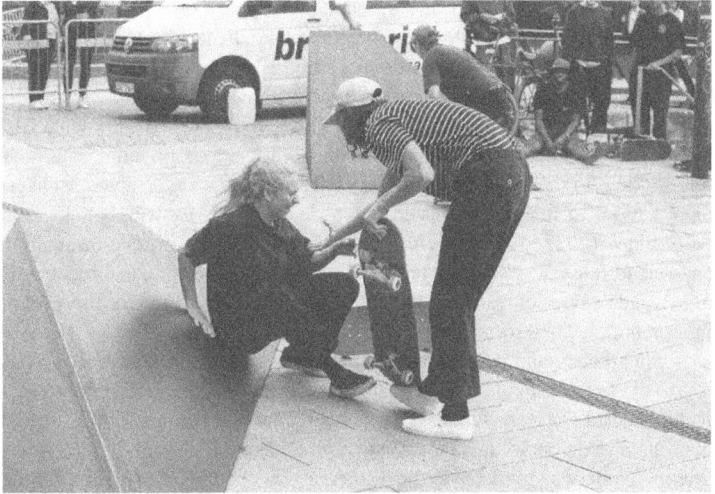

Figure 4.2 Helena Long offering help after a slam.
Source: Photo by Norma Ibarra.

neoliberal and masculine trophy or a dialectic between pleasure and pain (Halberstam 2011). Rather, failure is situated as a communal praxis: while a skater tumbles by themselves, the meaning of the fall depends on the joy or fear instilled by one's surrounding community. For Alexa, a trans woman, this means not fearing to fail because her environment supports her for who she is. Rather than a spiritual journey of the individual, failure here assumes the meaning of solidarity and care, facilitating a process of personal growth beyond trick acquisition.

Instead of stabilizing a skater's identity by landing a trick (or bailing to do so at a larger-than-life skateable obstacle), *Transenders* proposes failure as a phenomenology of care. There is a socio-historical necessity for this reconfiguration: "it was primarily men running the core industry (...) circulating the narratives of 'authenticity' that favored risk-taking" (Beal and Ebeling 2019: 102). This "masculine entrenchment" positions the *gnarly* skater as a neuter: failure equates to untapped pleasure, a source for neoliberal self-improvement, a testing ground for one's resilience – a claim that *this is skateboarding*.

Slow is not soft

SLAG pushes the notion of care in other ways, too. In the early 2020s, the organization introduced a slogan previously unknown in skate culture: "Skate slow and live." This tagline featured on a hoodie sold to raise additional funds, as much as it marketed a podcast by Save the Redwoods League – centering on a sleepaway skate camp in the Sequoia National Forest, California (I'll Go if You Go 2022). While the slogan's potential meanings are manifold, its origins are clear-cut: this is a direct response to *Skate or Die*. The slogan targets divergent groups of skaters by proposing that skateboarding is not just one thing. It is plural, intimating: *these are skateboardings!* What's suggested is that skateboarding transcends the individualist praxis of falling and getting back up in the face of increasingly taller and longer skateable obstacles: there's more to it than fast-paced spectacle and pain. Bethany Geckle and Sally Shaw (2022: 137) analyze this kind of skater-led critique through an analysis of queerness: "Queer failure is not meant to be softened, recovered, or salvaged as perseverance in pursuit of triumph. It is failure for the sake of failure, unredeemed by success."

Rather than zooming in on failure as a stepping stone toward success, it has layers of meaning in and of itself. It can point toward the prefigurative idea that the world can be different: it is "a hopeful act of imagining, inspiring and building alternative futures rather than reproducing the present. Failure in the present is one way to discover those alternatives and lay a foundation for the future" (Geckle and Shaw 2022: 134). Failure can be inspiring, and not just by being resolved in the future through the successful landing of tricks and reaffirmation of one's skater's identity. Take Bryggeriet, a Malmö-based high school where students can take skateboarding as a class (and, stronger yet, as a major). In a panel discussion at skate conference *Pushing Boarders* (2019), vice principal John Dahlquist shares how skateboarding has instilled in Bryggeriet students an appreciation of trying. He says, "At the end of my classes, I usually have to throw my students out of the classroom. A lot of them beg for three more tries: *I've got this, just give me three more tries. I promise I will learn.*" Rather than considering academic failure as a catastrophic event, Dahlquist's students see the parallel with skateboarding: learning means trying, and at times you need more than one attempt to make it work. Moreover, they cheer each other on, acknowledging that each skater (and student) operates at a different level and faces a distinct challenge.

This is similar to what Alexa is referring to in the *Transenders* video when she draws connections between falling/failing and community: what's at stake is a collective effort by non-traditional skaters to take their claim to an identity relevant within a historically exclusionary industry. Reappropriating failure means imagining what else skateboarding – and our broader societal structures – could be. It is to say, *there must be a better way*. Crucially, such a representation of failure is not located outside of the axes of hegemonic skateboarding. Precisely by producing the film *Transenders* in close collaboration with Nike, SLAG aims to achieve social transformation against the dark and problematic backdrop of neoliberalism. It problematizes the binary of sportification as *bad* and grassroots as *good*, critically engaging the complexity of global capitalism – and perhaps even realizing there might not be a viable alternative for the economy of skateboarding.

Considering how failure in skateboarding is interpreted and ritualized complicates a totalistic understanding of the sensory experience of riding a board. This shift from *Skate and Destroy* and *Skate or Die* to *Skate Slow and Live* orbits contrasting features such as hard versus soft skills, high performance versus collectivist sensibilities, grit versus care, resilience versus respect, meritocracy versus grassroots cooperation. Consider these words by professional skater Elissa Steamer, "I heard somebody saying that, as a woman or a girl, they were scared to go to a skatepark full of guys. So, why would you just go skate somewhere else – where there wasn't a bunch of guys? (…) So you could get more comfortable on a skateboard and then maybe return to the skatepark" (Pushing Boarders 2018; see also, Abulhawa 2020). In response, panel host Jilleen Liao asks, "Why isn't the skatepark more inclusive? Why do they have to turn around and go somewhere else?" While Steamer argues she's never experienced exclusivity in skateparks, she did do so elsewhere: "I was a child, like eleven or twelve, and there was a ramp up the street from my house, a little wooden mini ramp. And I went there to skate with my friends and we had a great time, we were skating. And then I went back a day or two later and (…) written on the ramp was, 'Skater Bettys Don't Swallow' (…) I knew that a skater Betty was a girl skater, you know, and I knew it was directed at me, because my friends were not telling me what it meant when I asked, *what does it mean*?"

Rather than resolving such binaries, a video like *Transenders* – contrasted with Steamer's commentary on misogyny – legitimizes the proliferation of the plural *skateboardings*. It is a prefiguration that there's no need to learn to skate in your own backyard before turning to the male-dominated, intimidating, and high-performance skateparks. But it also implies that there are no *illegal* or *undesirable* ways of sideways movement: this reconfiguration of the politics, symbolism, and expressive qualities of divergent performances and tricks aims to foster a more welcoming cultural environment. Reconsidering what skateboarding should look like means questioning its historical motifs of self-reliance and the hustle, by imagining an alternative future and finding joy and hope in the process of doing so. Reappropriating failure reveals that "other ways of being are possible" by "refusing conventional norms (…) as much as it is an unwillingness to adhere to hegemonic terms of success" (Geckle 2021: 206).

To say that it's okay to skate slow and live implies that there's more to skateboarding than the mastery of movement over time, to the bounty of failure in the lead-up to success, and to the neoliberal notion of the self-made man. Like switch stance, failure can be part of a skater's orientation, showcasing their outlook on the world. Here, skateboarding operates as a pedagogy of minor falls, neither shying away from failure nor celebrating it as a token of self-reliance or meritocracy. Instead, failure becomes an emancipatory and future-oriented tool: it operates as a fingerprint, perhaps even a signature – disclosing the values and personality of the skater on display.

References

Abulhawa, D. (2020). *Skateboarding and Femininity: Gender, Space-Making and Expressive Movement*. London: Routledge.

Bäckström, Å. (2013). "Gender Manoeuvring in Swedish Skateboarding: Negotiations of Femininities and the Hierarchical Gender Structure." *Young*, 21.1: 29–53.

Beachy, K. (2021). *The Most Fun Thing: Dispatches from a Skateboard Life*. New York: Grand Central Publishing.

Beal, B., & Ebeling, K. (2019). "Can You Sell Out If You've Never Been in." In Schwier, J., & Kilberth, V. (eds.). *Skateboarding Between Subculture and the Olympics*, 97–113. Bielefeld: Transcript.

Buckareff, A. (2021). "Sisyphus, Skateboarders, and the Value in Endless Failure." *Psyche* 1 December 2021, https://psyche.co/ideas/sisyphus-skateboarders-and-the-value-in-endless-failure.

Cheng, D. (2022). "Transenders." *Nike SB and Skate Like a Girl*, https://www.youtube.com/watch?v=Be_wn0EjzJQ.

Corwin, Z. B., Williams, N., Maruco, T., & Romero-Morales, M. (2019). *Beyond the Board: Skateboarding, Schools, and Society*. Pullias Center for Higher Education.

Dixon, D. (2011). "Getting the Make: Japanese Skateboarder Videography and the Entranced Ethnographic Lens." *Postmodern Culture* 22.1: online, https://muse.jhu.edu/article/481022.

Dreyfus, H. L. (1991). *Being-in-the-World*. Cambridge: MIT Press.

Dupont, T. (2014). "From core to Consumer: The Informal Hierarchy of the Skateboard Scene." *Journal of Contemporary Ethnography*, 43.5: 556–581.

Geckle, B. (2021). *Queer World-making: Destabilizing Heteronormativity through Skateboarding*. University of Otago: PhD Thesis.

Geckle, B., & Shaw, S. (2022). "Failure and Futurity: The Transformative Potential of Queer Skateboarding." *Young*, 30.2: 132–148.

Emerica. (2003). *This is Skateboarding*, 46 min, https://www.youtube.com/watch?v=wkvwxVt3jI0.

Halberstam, J. (2011). *The Queer Art of Failure*. Durham: Duke University Press.

Harris, A. (2020). *A Sensory Education*. London: Routledge.

Hölsgens, S. (2018a). "Towards the Spatial Affectivities of Colour: The Blue Bedroom in Yasujirō Ozu's an Autumn Afternoon." In Rosário, F., & Villarmea Álvarez, I. (eds.). *New Approaches to Cinematic Space*, 205–215. London: Routledge.

Hölsgens, S. (2021). *Skateboarding in Seoul: A Sensory Ethnography*. Groningen: University of Groningen Press.

Hölsgens, S., & O'Connor, P. (2022). "Traces of Failure in Skateboarding Videos." *Flow Journal* 28.4: online, https://www.flowjournal.org/2022/02/failure-in-skateboarding/.

Howes, D. (2023). *Sensorial Investigations: A History of the Senses in Anthropology, Psychology, and Law*. Pennsylvania: The University of Pennsylvania Press.

Huizinga, J. (2008). *Homo ludens: proeve eener bepaling van het spel-element der cultuur*. Amsterdam: Amsterdam University Press.

I'll Go if You Go. (2022). Skate Slow & Live. In: *A Save the Redwoods League Podcast*, https://open.spotify.com/episode/6StCABddHisRt63J4T2dra?.

Kim, K. (2013). *Unsung #6*. Seoul: Moonsung Printing.

Low, K. E. (2015). "The Sensuous City: Sensory Methodologies in Urban Ethnographic Research." *Ethnography*, 16.3: 295–312.

Nike. (2022). *Skate Like a Girl*, https://www.nikesb.com/articles/skate-like-a-girl, last accessed 19 March 2024.
O'Connor, P. (2019). *Skateboarding and Religion*. Berlin: Springer Nature.
Pushing Boarders. (2018). *Heavy Discussion Presents: Concrete Waves and The Rise of Female Skaters*, https://www.youtube.com/watch?v=rpGpPOsAOgQ&, last accessed 19 March 2024.
Pushing Boarders. (2019). *Skate & Educate: From Classrooms to Communities*, https://www.youtube.com/watch?v=COAx2zVnwtY, last accessed 19 March 2024.
Robinson, J. (2021). "Olympic Skateboarding's Helmet Headache." *The Wall Street Journal*, 4 August 2021, https://www.wsj.com/articles/olympic-skateboard-helmet-headache-11628060689.
Skate Like a Girl. (online). *Our Mission*, https://www.skatelikeagirl.com/about.html, last accessed on 10 July 2024.
SLS. (2024). *2023 SLS Super Crown São Paulo: Women's FINAL*, https://www.youtube.com/watch?v=WQptXOVztZU, last accessed 19 March 2024.
The Berrics. (2018). Heath Kirchart's Battle Scars, https://www.youtube.com/watch?v=ax-rP3wZQyE, last accessed 19 March 2024.
Vadi, J. (2022). "More Joy and Less Cool What it means to be a skater." *The Yale Review*, 1 March 2022, https://yalereview.org/article/jos%C3%A9-vadi-skateboarding-streets.
Vice. (2022). "From Skating to Death-Defying Travel Missions: Heath Kirchart | Epicly Later'd," https://www.youtube.com/watch?v=Cd7txJozAWw.
Webb, M. (2024). *Break Point*, https://www.netflix.com/title/81569920.
Williams, N. (2022). "Before the Gold: Connecting Aspirations, Activism, and BIPOC Excellence through Olympic Skateboarding." *Journal of Olympic Studies*, 3.1: 4–27.
Willing, I., & Pappalardo, A. (2023). *Skateboarding, Power and Change*. Berlin: Springer.
Zero. (1997). *Thrill of it all*, 22 min, https://www.youtube.com/watch?v=oHAgpF12rPA.

5 Grey Pleasure
Skateboarding as a Deviant and Salubrious Ecology

Skateboarding escapes the piercing tendency to equate new with better. Since the 1980s, a skateboard's main features have been layers of hard maple laminate screwed to two aluminum trucks, on which ball bearings, inserted into four polyurethane wheels, are bolted. The Sony VX1000 has been "skating's favorite camera" since its introduction in 1995 (Coles 2020). Combined with the MK Ultra fisheye lens, the VX communicates an aesthetic of low-fi cool and a nostalgic sensibility for a time that once was. High-prized competitions still work with judges, usually retired professionals, whose assessments are opaque, mysterious, and at times scolded (Blum 2016). Unlike social and technological developments in other sports – such as video refereeing in football, high-performance attire in track and field, and data analytics in basketball – progress in skateboarding is astoundingly conservative. This technological traditionalism sparks a question once posed by critic Kyle Beachy (2021: 203): "Is skateboarding a primitive force, or is it a progressive one?"

Skateboarding's stagnate materialism shadows its social progress. Its principle tool – the board – is increasingly seen as multipurpose, having "the capacity to mediate human relations to the world in multiple ways" (Rosenberger 2018: 175). Beyond athletic performance, a skateboard is a pluralist tool for creativity (Chiu and Giamarino 2019), social good (Radikonyana et al. 2017), pedagogy (Romero 2020), spirituality (O'Connor 2019), and performativity (Abulhawa 2020). It's no surprise that sports associations, nongovernmental organizations (NGOs), educational institutions, landscape architects, and city councils want in. Entrusting skaters to change the world for the better, cities including Malmö, Bordeaux, and Seoul translate such positive assessments into skate-friendly policies (Hölsgens 2024).

But friendly to whom: practitioners, the city, the environment? That is the subject of our concluding chapter: how the skaters' admiration of urban spaces corresponds to discourses of friendliness and hostility. At once benign and harmful, we argue that skateboarding has the potential of foregrounding health and wellness in the polluting environs of urban space. What emerges are sensitive landscapes – at once joyful and toxic, full of deviance and care,

DOI: 10.4324/9781003510642-5
This chapter has been made available under a CC-BY-NC-ND 4.0 license.

affectively alienating and profoundly familiar. These landscapes reverberate a buffet of sensory experiences, enacting a range of traits from grit to spiritual resolution, and ultimately push toward a multispecies futurity.[1]

Perceptive ecologies

Navigating a damaged planet, skaters insert ludic and enskiled meaning onto the ruins of the Anthropocene, finding fulfillment in the hardpan surfaces of the city. Their pleasure is due to these polluting materialities in their built environments, located at fuming city centers and marginalized industrial spaces. A skater's tacit knowledge is a ludic activity enmeshed in materially and socially polluted spaces of urban detritus (cf. O'Connor et al. 2023; Willing and Pappalardo 2023). We take as a given that "skateboarders must work *with* the materialities of pollution alongside social critique that they are themselves pollutants if they are to harness spaces of capitalism for ludic purposes" (O'Connor et al. 2023: 898). This conceptualization denotes the specification of the monochromatic city, the (un)desired social position of skaters, and the culture's coincidental entanglements with environmental damage and toxicity.

The contrasting grey space of the city with its surrounding green (or blue) ecology advances the idea that skaters experience limited salubrious effects from their favored environs. Skateboarding exists at the margins of regular sports activities, most of which tend to be performed in purpose-built, safe, and increasingly sustainable spatialities (Wergeland and Hognestad 2021). To see this difference, consider the spaces of sport: baseball is played in its field, American football in its stadium, swimming in its pool, and basketball on its court. Increasingly, we might say that skateboarding is also played in its park, a mainstream sport facility mimicking street furniture in purpose-built environs (Glenney and O'Connor 2019; Hölsgens 2021). Such facilities are constructed according to agreed architectural dimensions and progressively cater to the desire for circular design for observation by non-participating fans. These sites – usually found in city parks or suburban greeneries – define the sport, providing a consistent basis for a sport's athletic achievement in its common quest for human excellence (Simon et al. 2015: 47). These parks are thus painted with the health and wellbeing observed in recreational spaces of salubrity (Clark and Sayers 2023).

By contrast, the spatial contours of unregulated leisure activities are variegated and unpredictable. Surfers must adapt to their changing blue, oceanic space, including weather and wave conditions, swell, wind, tide, and even shark predation. Mountain bikers must shift balance in their green, hilly space among elevated conditions like wind and rain, mud and dust, and eroding terrains. And rally drivers must seek the limits between road and off-road, drawing attention to the boundaries between the built and the wild. Leisure activities occurring in blue and green spaces have additional benefits, intrinsic salubrious effects that support participant health and wellbeing via ecological features including microbiota (Potter et al. 2023). To engage in physical activity among other living organisms is one of the principal reasons for the renewed popularity of surfing and mountain biking, marked by their recent inclusion in the Olympic Games. Beyond competitive sports, these activities are increasingly seen as part of a green, sustainable, healthy lifestyle.

In the context of the Anthropocene and late capitalism, physical activity among nonhuman life is intoxicating and problematic. Surfing regularly takes place in postindustrial coastal regions, an extreme yet by no means unique example of which are the irradiated waters behind concrete seawalls in Fukushima (Evers 2019; 2021). What's more, the 2008 Olympic Games in Beijing gave prominence to the ramifications of air pollution on marathon runners, including how women are disproportionately affected by environmental toxicity (Marr and Ely 2010). Skiers and snowboarders face snowless mountains as a result of global warming and climate change, threatening biodiversity in alpine areas (cf. Konvicka et al. 2021; Stoddart 2011). The excess of ambient air pollution, carbon dioxide, microplastics, and other toxins render any outdoor leisure activity as potentially insalubrious. "Any accretion of health and well-being," surf scholar Clifton Evers (2021: 179) writes, "is shown to simultaneously involve declension, within immediate and/or distant proximity." Surfers and mountain bikers have a front-row view of environmental degradation, debunking the illusion that the grass is still green and water is still blue. Unregulated leisure activities reveal the truth of an underlying pollution and disease, a dysbiosis in the spaces of salubrity. What's won is immediately lost.

This growing recognition for anthropogenic toxins in the context of leisure and sports activities deepens our understanding of how practitioners *live with* and *attend to* pollution. This is recently conceptualized as "polluted" and "sensitive" leisure (cf. Evers 2019; Zajchowski and Rose 2020). This typology of leisure is especially relevant for skateboarding, not least because it takes place in environments marked by their austere urban skin: concrete, tarmac, and steel (Potter et al. 2023). Besides the grey space of city centers, abandoned brownfields and Superfund sites make for some of the most pleasurable and fetishized skate spots. These urban sites are particularly hostile because of a looming pollution both material and social, suggesting that grey, skateable space is fundamentally harmful – perhaps even more so than the oceanic spaces of surfers. Thus, skateboarding exists in a conundrum. Its salubrious clime – its fertile flora and fauna – is a dysbiotic environment: out-of-balance, injurious, and destructive. These environmental conditions are matched by a social toxicity revealed when skateboarding confronts the dominant socio-aesthetic orders of the city (Glenney 2024).

Still, skaters somehow find benefits in their craft: recent scholarship strongly suggests the existence of salubrious health and wellbeing effects in skateboarding (Corwin et al. 2019). This shift to salubrity is pronounced in the growing areas of adaptive skating and WCMX (Wheel Chair Moto Cross), which adapt tricks from skateboarding and BMX. As Darryl, a WCMX rider quipped, "the wheelchair doesn't have to be a medical device, it can be something fun" (Dean 2023: 110) Skateboards also disrupt concepts of medical mobility, with several skaters mentioning how its initial use as transport unfolds in a lifestyle identity over their life course. Toni, a Brazilian born with a rare genetic disease preventing normal leg growth, has been on a skateboard since he was three. "Like the skateboard was always the way that I used to walk. I was always on a skateboard. This was the first bond. I knew that it was like my legs. Like the skateboard is my legs" (Dean 2023: 100).

Visually impaired skaters also found immense social empowerment through skateboarding, often using white canes as a guide. As VI skater Matt states, "Like we're all using skateboarding as an identity in a world that doesn't give an identity to blind people. That doesn't give the forethought to give blind people the time and space to allow them to be fully realized humans and skateboarding does that" (Dean 2023: 103). Because skateboarding is more than a sport, adaptive skaters' sense of wellbeing, health, and empowerment seems to correlate more with their community and crafting personal betterment than formal competition, winning, and other sporting motifs. Such experiences push the argument that skateboarding holds the potential for salubrity, though kinesiologist Nikolaus Dean (2023: 106) notes how these are conditioned by "the intersection of gender and disability" – resulting in fewer opportunities and less recognition for women.

What exactly could be at the core of skateboarding as a salubrious activity, given its socio-ecological greyness? A recent distinction has been suggested between active and passive participation (Holt et al. 2019), and more broadly, direct and indirect participation with green and blue spaces (Jarosz 2023). Direct sunlight and moving through nature, rather than indirect viewing through a window at a distance, increase environmental benefits (Turunen et al. 2023). What's more, engaging in physical activity in green and blue spaces, like running and cycling, intensifies its salubrious effects, as opposed to sitting and picnicking (Holt et al. 2019). Forest bathing and meditative walking practices are examples of even greater attentive inspection and inspiration from these natural spaces, further increasing health and wellbeing. Hence, while green and blue spaces offer prime conditions for beneficial physical and psychological effects, it is the directness and interactivity of their use that seem requisite for their acquisition.

While theories of how green and blue spaces produce health and wellbeing abound, it remains unclear which specific processes are involved and whether they are different across this spectrum of encounter. Perhaps these processes are grounded in the production of spaces: forest bathing creates a heightened sensory clime through enskiled strategies of directly using greens and blues. What's at stake is physical health: improved air quality, temperature regulation, and the freeing possibilities of open spaces. There are also secondary psychological benefits of stress and anxiety reduction that come from direct engagement with greens and blues, as well as social benefits of community interaction, such as hikes and camping trips with friends. Finally, these embodied and emplaced opportunities to more fully engage biodiverse climes and experience biophilia form deeper human/nonhuman interactions. While the evidence that supports these claims remains preliminary, as there is no standard methodology available, making studies often confounding, mixed, and heterogeneous (Gascon et al. 2015; Geneshka et al. 2021), these are profoundly hopeful and are practiced in various kinds of medical and therapeutic care.

Parallel to the distinction between passive, active, and interactive engagement with spaces of leisure, a spectrum of green, blue, and grey craft emerges. Occupational therapists recommend somatic and kinesthetic strategies of forest bathing and horticulture therapy that include breathing exercises, gardening practices, and taking in sensory stimuli: the smells, sounds, and sights of the diverse and living ecologies (Stepansky et al. 2023). These salubrity strategies may be important for unlocking these otherwise secreted or latent benefits. This is correlated with issues of spatial justice: the distribution of blue and green spaces is uneven in quality and quantity. Access to the best spaces often reserved for wealthy areas of the city that can afford to plan and maintain such spaces.

When discussing greens and blues in cities, most attention goes to planned or preservation design for a more livable city – ponds, parks, allotment gardens, trails, street trees, canals, and courtyards. Consider the example of street trees, which illustrate how managed greens play central to skateboarding's grey craft. Sociologist Duncan McDuie-Ra (2022) presents a trinity of reasons that street trees planted in pavement by cities: to green up grey urban infrastructure, provide shade for citizens, and control use of specific structures by placing potted plants on ledges to keep skaters (and other unwanted users) away. For skaters, street trees are like curbs and stairs, representing incredible possibilities. They are an "X" that the city marks as a spot ripe for skateboarding. Their roots lift pavement to provide inclines and bumps for trick play. The structural artifices bordering street trees, ledges and curbs, often present ideal conditions for skateboarding tricks.

In a word, skaters may not be fully alienated from nature but find it on every turn and push. Their knowledge of and care for the city are not unlike a mushroom hunter's ability to attune to human-distributed forests (cf. Hölsgens 2021; Tsing 2015): both attend to a complex, multi-layered, and greyish ecology against the backdrop of industrialization and late capitalism. Their enskilment includes more than a simple quest for value (i.e. skateable space and edible fungi); it's a distinctive relationality to their socio-ecological environments. Street trees present a natural ally to skateboarding's own unruly behavior: no architecture can contain street trees, while skaters cannot be tamed and kept within their spaces.

Figure 5.1 Perry Tomczyk, an adaptive skater from Burlington, Vermont, skates sitting on his board with his legs bent to the sides.

Source: Photo by Brian Glenney.

Deviant craft

Skaters reappropriate the property of others for ludic and creative purposes, subverting its intended use-case (Borden 2001). For this reason, skateboarding is often portrayed as a deviant type of leisure, constructing an altersociality of urban infrastructure (cf. Dickinson et al. 2022; McDuie-Ra 2022).

Consider the example of the Dolores Street Hill Bomb in San Francisco. An annual unregulated event, its exact dates are announced a few days prior in an attempt to avoid disruption by police (Barros 2023). The event brings together hundreds of skaters, some of whom skate down Dolores Street's Liberty hill – one of the city's steepest inclines.

Challenging its intended use of safe transportation for cars, motorcycles, and bicycles, skaters thwart its design by speeding from top to bottom. As skateboards have neither brakes nor engines, and thus do not fall under licensing jurisdiction, they are disorderly machines in themselves. Skaters use hills like Dolores Street to propel at velocity for risky play, helmetless. Injuries at the Hill Bomb are frequent (Barros 2023), creating a recreational "Jackass" spectacle out of this otherwise banal space for transportation (Willing et al. 2023). Cultivating a potential health crisis from the perspective of the city, police intervention was deemed necessary in recent years (Glenney 2024). The director of the parks department, a "veteran skater himself," has gone on record claiming that he believes it would be green-lit (Barros 2023). And yet, part and parcel of this leisure use of Dolores Street – perhaps what makes it deviant – is that skaters do not apply for a permit to sanction the downhill event.

San Francisco's concreted hills are objects of fascination for other wheel-based activities, too: both fixed-gear cycling and low-riding tricycles frequently win city permits to protest in support of spatial justice initiatives (Barros 2023). But skaters do it differently, performing deviant acts not for road access or safe transportation but for its own sake: for leisure. As the late skater Zane Timpson says in a report by *The New Yorker* (Jonassen and Holmes 2021): "Bombing is, like, going fast, feeling the wind, feeling the board rumble on the asphalt, just getting past that point of any return. You are giving yourself to the speed […] It's such a freedom." An alternative to staccato trick play, which is punctuated by repeated trial-and-error, hill bombing is legato: uninterruptedly skating at high speeds, where escaping failure is a necessity for survival. Rather than an opportunity to learn tricks, falling during a hill bomb equates to an injury. Here, progress is made by *not falling*, by staying upright.

Instead of purposeful transportation, hill bombers experience the San Francisco streets as a "holy or unholy place" cultivating a sense of freedom (Jonassen and Holmes 2021). But the pursuit of freedom increasingly comes at the cost of deviant or illegal behavior. In 2020, the city installed raised pavements dots: hostile architecture that prevents small-wheeled machines from using the streets (*CBS News* 2020). In 2023, the event led to a mass arrest of over 100 skaters, and many have attempted to sue the police department (Barros 2023). This motivated the Dolores Street neighborhood to voice their support of the police's use of force to stop the event. We find, for instance, Dolores Street resident Bob Bathrick in an email asking, "Is this a protest? Skaters – is there a message you are trying to tell society with this Hill Bomb? If so, what is it?" (SFPD Commission 2023, Bob Bathrick).

What makes this event difficult to comprehend is that there is no clear message or aim. The Hill Bombers' non-traditional use of the streets is about their leisure, viewing the city as a "deviant playground" (McDuie-Ra 2022: 51). The Dolores Street Hill Bomb is an activity that cannot easily be commodified, or perhaps not at all. Rather than neatly separating work from nonwork via purpose-built playgrounds or beaches or gyms, hill bombs position pleasure where it is least wanted: on streets predominantly used by motorized vehicles traversing between domestic and office spaces. By alienating themselves from socio-economic discourse, skaters even succeed in escaping the tenets of the leisure industry: centering *pleasure* on the purpose-built tarmac of the streets means negating capitalist structures of domination and commodification.

To some, the Hill Bomb is a clear case of skate crime, antagonizing the neighborhood for their own thrill-seeking pleasure. Local resident Bathrick adds that the Hill Bomb has real social harm: "we have 10 years of data that shows the physical and psychological degradation of the neighborhood and its residents at these events" (SFPD Commission 2023, Bob Bathrick). The purported social harm is unlike that of individual violent criminal behavior. Rather, it seems to orbit the promotion of antisocial behavior by skate culture itself. For criminologists Oliver Smith and Thomas Raymen (2018), deviant leisure constitutes a specific form of social harm by eroding beneficial social values. The disabuse of safety is one obvious example of a socially beneficial value negated by skate crime: most hill bombers eschew the use of helmets, even though concussions are common and traumatic brain injury is a known risk (Mitchao et al. 2022).

Observing skaters engaged in careless risk may be a form of "psychological degradation," as suggested by Bob Bathrick, one likened to observing open drug use, public drinking, and other illicit acts. A more sociological analysis reveals some of the accusations of the social harm of the Hill Bomb as a kind of "not in my back yard" (NIMBY) reaction. To the Dolores Street residents, skaters are from a comparatively lower-class demographic. Residents in the Mission-Dolores neighborhood have a median income of \$181.000, with Dolores Street homes valued at a median of \$2 million, perhaps helping to account for their antagonism toward the annual skate event (*City-Data. Com* 2021). This NIMBY interpretation gains strength by considering how skateboarding's socio-aesthetic order of its spaces might be viewed from a class sensibility: a product of the poor who cannot afford their own spaces.

And yet, the Hill Bomb is part of the rich cultural heritage of Dolores Street: it celebrates one of the steepest hills in San Francisco, showing their ecological literacy and concern by paying homage to the green-grey landscape. The Dolores Street Hill Bomb as a community-building event celebrates the architectural and infrastructural marvel of Liberty Hill. What's more, by demonstrating how this alternative use of the built environment challenges uneven access to public space, skaters perform the change they want to see in the world – a prefigurative politics. They are subverters of just landscaped grey or concreted green, critiquing the polluting surfaces of the streets and the dominance of combustion engines. But they also challenge social grey, where "participation, horizontality, and inclusion combine as a strategy for molding a world accessible and sympathetic to the lifestyle of skateboarders" (idem: 40). Their main ingredients are pleasure and risk.

A hill bomber's assessment of risk is more phenomenal than analytic, as Zane Timpson confirms:

> Timing traffic lights is important. It's a little bit more of a guessing game, but if you pay enough attention, you can find the patterns and you can assess risk and be able to go down when it is most likely that you will be able to have a clear path. It's dangerous. It's scary.
>
> (Jonassen and Holmes 2021)

Though most injuries are no worse than some bruises and scratches, skaters have been whisked away from Dolores Street in ambulances with head injuries, including one fatality (Barros 2023). Not unlike free climbers, hill bombers put everything on the line for a good run, increasing what Langseth and Salvesen (2018) call a "risk libido." By bombing the steepest hills at the highest possible speeds, skaters accumulate symbolic capital. The higher the risk, the greater the recognition. This is another tacit understanding skaters hold of the toxic city – intimately knowing the damage grey spaces can do to the human body. Risk assessment, here, is interwoven with the hurting knowledge of failure and the damaging qualities of the modern city: it is a *grey pleasure* against the backdrop of a more-than-human landscape.

Commodified pleasure

Lacking proper brakes, hill bombers intermittently try to slow down by powersliding – turning the board sideways while moving forward. It's a technique similar to creating a wedge while skiing or skidding on a brakeless bike, the main difference being its efficacy. On straight surfaces or regular slopes, powerslides are a useful means for slowing down. However, the small size of a skateboard's polyurethane wheels limit the brake force of powerslides: despite being turned 90 degrees, there is insufficient friction between the wheels and the tarmac to sufficiently decelerate when skating steep slopes like Liberty Hill. What's more, the wheels generate enormous heat because of their accelerated, if not violent, contact with the streets' surface. Overheating wheels makes it all the more difficult to twist and turn, let alone at speeds of twenty to thirty miles per hour, as is the case in hill bombing.

As such, powerslides are more an aesthetic performance than an effective tool – being one of the few instances where the characteristic sideways stance makes way for a forward-facing technique. While bombing hills, facing forward could be interpreted as a zero-degree aesthetic, an embodied interface for skaters to re-examine their disorderly position within the world. Against the backdrop of San Francisco's mountains and hills, a powerslide is a brief and tense moment during which skaters are acutely aware of the impossibility to escape danger: while roads are designed to tame landscapes and create a (faux) sense of safety, Hill Bombs offer an alternative to dominant cultural orders – showing the aesthetic and unpredictable relationality between human and nonhuman life. Rather than yet another natural phenomenon to dominate, Liberty Hill is an active agent in the skater's process of producing space, of crafting the city, and of negotiating freedom. Moving beyond the point of no return by achieving a speed beyond control, skaters give themselves to their landscapes, taking pleasure in their grey craft of risk-taking.

For Marxist philosopher Henri Lefebvre (2014), a concrete utopia begins with *jouissance*, with pleasure and joy, offering imaginaries radically different from capitalist work and other "useful" activities. Linking pleasure to physical and moral wellbeing, Lefebvre draws attention to the difference between work and nonwork. While work is encapsulated in productivist discourse, nonwork is "an activity that cannot be commodified" (Lefebvre 2014: xix). At Dolores Street, skateboarding is not reducible to the value of use. It intentionally breaks away from the use-value purpose of transit and even commodified exchange-value of leisure spaces, both of which equate to car use benefiting the automobile or gasoline industry. These industrial activities – including the sonic terror of motorized vehicles and the stench of burnt fuel – are acceptable because of the value they bring.

Despite being recognized as a source of *environmental* pollution, cars escape the critique of being a form of *social* pollution, for their drivers take part in value production within a decidedly capitalist society. So, skating for pleasure, for the pure sake of it, engenders a political and even activist stance, performing an enskiled critique of the city's socio-legal configurations. Similar to activist biking events, the Hill Bomb could function as an intervention, arguing for fair road share. But unlike biking activism, a Hill Bomb event could never be sanctioned, as the very aesthetic of the space is made in its illegal reappropriation for a use that it was not intended for: risky pleasure that sacralizes mountainous landscapes (O'Connor 2019). For San Francisco skaters, Liberty Hill is marked by the landscape's wondrous shapes and sizes: their more-than-human slopes hold a spiritual and almost existential meaning, merging an aesthetic homage to a greyified city with the risky sensory experience of hill bombing.

While modernist architecture and urban planning may generate classist ideology, skateboarding shreds it asunder. The Dolores Street hill is for skaters what the boulevards, designed by Georges-Eugène Haussmann, were to the Parisian working class in the late nineteenth century: a socio-spatial opportunity to reappropriate urban spaces designed for the wealthy and powerful. In doing so, skaters make painfully clear how space is socially constructed. While tax-funded streets are said to be a social equilibrium – being accessible, useful, and meaningful to anyone – the hill bombs amplify their built-in undercurrents. For a few hours, the streets belong to skaters, whose hill bombs subvert the false narrative of road safety and shared access. Like the crass lyrics and noisy debauchery of punk music, calling attention to the even more egregious horrors of nuclear war, corporate theft of fair housing, and medical treatments, the skater's shrieking trespasses reveal underlying privatizing codes of public spaces. As Howell (2001: 64) notes, "skateboarding is exceptionally good at drawing attention to the quietly exclusionary nature of the new public space."

The discourse of social pollution through skateboarding's unwanted acts looks quite different in the context of craft (Chapter 3): rather than mindless deviance, it offers a space for performing progressive social critique. We can shift the tables and observe how the dysbiosis caused by the Dolores Street Hill Bomb is more due to the reactionary response from the neighbors and city police and its dominant order. If skateboarding were a celebrated *cultural* activity, the Dolores Street neighborhood might recognize the meaning and value of the event, welcoming it as a parade, a carnival of carnage to whoop and maybe get walloped. Skaters who antagonize a municipality's written and unwritten codes through its craft may accidentally or actively rewrite its arbitrary rules, ones that are more spatially and socially just.

Simultaneously, the risk of becoming good and compliant partners to the city is the inescapable undercurrent of gentrification. Ocean Howell (2008: 485) observes that city councils use skaters as unwitting troops for urban renewal since their presence "can deter vandalism, drug use, prostitution, and homeless encampments" (Howell 2008: 485). Deeply encapsulated in gentrification strategies, skateboarding is part of urban managers' "toolkit for the revitalization of poor and former industrial areas" (ibid). More recently, Max Harrison-Caldwell (2023) notes how the San Francisco Recreation and Park Department (SFRPD) announced a "two-year experimental skate plaza" at United Nations Plaza, just two days after the massive arrest of over 100 skaters at the Dolores Street Hill Bomb. The plaza is notorious for its open drug use, dealing, and homeless encampments. As much as skateboarding itself is criminalized and stigmatized, it also operates as an ignorant stakeholder to get rid of unwanted social groups. Grey pleasure, in other words, is a two-edged sword: it instills an opportunity to make public space more welcoming to creativity and nonwork, positioning skateboarding as an emancipatory tool, as much as it is a catalyst for advancing socio-economic segregation.

Urban historian and former professional skater Ocean Howell calls skaters to recognize the social position they hold:

> Now that the cities are actually listening to us, I think it's important to be selective and not to just agree to anything. I'll use an exaggerated example to make the point: what if there was a site that was like a woman's health clinic, or like an orphanage or a homeless shelter, and they're like, 'we're going to level all this stuff, we're not providing any replacement services or anything but build a beautiful skatepark,' I think they should say no to that.
> (Harmon and Derrien 2018, online)

Howell's suggestion might be encapsulated in a case example of the proposed "leveling" of a beloved greenspace section in Mount Prospect Park in Brooklyn for a skatepark, designed by the Tony Hawk Foundation. Once a lookout station for George Washington's army, this space is set to be "one of the biggest skate parks on the East Coast" (Barron 2024, online). The local residents' concern seems valid, as "the poured-concrete skateboarding facility

Figure 5.2 Hunter Okano hefts a Texas Plant under Burnside Bridge in Portland, Oregon, one of the world's most iconic skateparks.

Source: Photo by Brian Glenney.

would take up precious green space in a city that does not have enough of it" (ibid). Here, commoning skateable space equates to de-greenification. So, skaters now have a say in the chromatic meaning of city space: green or grey?

Ecological enskilment

The differentiation between green and grey spaces is a socio-historical construct, as much as it is a physical reality. Acceptable greens are polished and well-maintained; wild growth – while factually *green* – belongs to the realm of the grey: the industrial, abandoned, neglected, disguised. There's, as Marte Qvenild (2014) puts it, "wanted and unwanted nature," as much as there is desired and despised skateable space (Vivoni 2009). As such, there is a parallel between spontaneous nature and skateboarding's deviant play: both are actively excluded from the visible parts of the built environment to the point of being condemned and criminalized. If anything, wild growth and the spontaneous uses of architecture by skaters are considered an "invasive proliferation" when not adhering to city policies and a dominant neoliberal socio-aesthetic order.

Further comparisons can be drawn: the microhabitats of wild spaces correspond to the microcosms of crafted, skateable space. Both hardly exceed the parameter of a couple of square meters, fostering a small-scale ecology noticed by few, actively attended to by fewer. What's needed for spontaneous trick play and wild growth is not purpose-built design or landscape architecture but pockets of unused or undervalued space: an abandoned container, a weirdly shaped ledge, a red California curb, and a leaning lamppost. These spots also correlate to the assertive presence of spontaneous growth of nature in the built environment – cultivating unforeseen imaginaries and socio-ecological resistance. As Amartya Deb (2023: xviii) writes, "Wild urban spaces may hold secrets waiting to be discovered (...) facilitat[ing] new imaginations, and possible encourage a greater connection of urban dwellers with nature."

Wild spaces denote the entanglements of spontaneous nature growth in neglected or underappreciated urban grey. These greens can be both salubrious and dangerous. While standing water on a street with a poor drainage system may cultivate excellent conditions for nonhuman life – ranging from mosses to insects – such "small scale-nature may be composed of plant species that are able to cause discomfort upon contact" (Deb 2023: 35). Similarly, weeds growing on top of ledges can contribute to a lower surface temperature, if ever so slightly, but may also be a breeding ground for invasive species. However, compared to monocultural greens – often planted and managed by municipalities – wild growth overwhelmingly represents a biodiversity usually neglected or unrecognized in the context of the built environment. Rather than a normative fabrication of urban ecologies alongside the lines of green/grey, clean/dirty, and healthy/unhealthy, we recognize that these interstitial spaces give space to nature's and society's suppressed undercurrent: here, there's possibility and hope for pluralism, spontaneity, and unregulated life.

Urban practitioners are acutely aware that wild grasses grow in close proximity to walls perfectly suitable for graffiti art and wallrides – pushing back against both commercialized art and imported, easy-to-maintain plant species. These actants have the skillset to intuitively discern the correlation between spontaneous nature and the generative potential for play. Sensorially, they "become with" nonhuman species with whom they share microhabitats in the built environment (Haraway 2013). Skaters engage in not just a polluted but a sensitive leisure (cf. Evers 2019; Zajchowski and Rose 2020), employing their senses to attend to the socio-ecological precarity of the world. Sensitivity, here, points toward the use "a diverse faculty of senses" (idem: 2), as much as it refers to an embodied attunement to precarious spatial-environmental milieus.

Through a sideways stance, skaters notice and form alliances with the advent of greys and the untamable greens of wild growth. Their sensorium pulsates with environmental awareness: forging unexpected alliances with the non-living and living others, the *friendliness* of their skateable environment is co-dependent on the spontaneity of urban ecologies. Their tacit knowledge of the city makes them sensors in a city in flux, witnessing the decline and blossoming of wild space (Myers 2017). While not necessarily conscious, skaters attend to the ecological features of the built environment. In so doing, they are sensorially attuned to industrialist ecodice and other modes of toxicity and poisoning – recognizing hope and creativity where others see none.

Note

1 Parts of this chapter are derived from or revised reflections on the paper "Skateboard crime and the pirating of urban space," published in *Crime Media Culture*. We have obtained written consent to do so.

References

Abulhawa, D. (2020). *Skateboarding and Femininity: Gender, Space-Making and Expressive Movement*. London: Routledge.

Barron, J. (2024). "In Brooklyn, a Fight Over Paving Parkland for Skateboarding." *The New York Times*, 29 February 2024, https://www.nytimes.com/2024/02/29/nyregion/skatepark-brooklyn-park-tony-hawk.html.

Barros, J. R. (2023). "Legalizing Dolores Hill Bomb Would Be Trivial, Veteran Skaters Say — and SF May Be Receptive." *Mission Local*, 19 July 2023, http://missionlocal.org/2023/07/legalizing-dolores-hill-bomb-would-be-trivial-say-veteran-skaters-and-san-francisco-may-be-receptive/.

Beachy, K. (2021). *The Most Fun Thing: Dispatches from a Skateboard Life*. New York: Grand Central Publishing.

Blum, S. (2016). "Is Street League Skateboarding a Sell-Out?" *Vice*, https://www.vice.com/en/article/mgzbzn/is-street-league-skateboarding-a-sell-out.

Borden, I. (2001). *Skateboarding, Space and the City: Architecture and the Body*. Oxford: Berg Publishers.

CBS News. (2020). "San Francisco Officials Move to Stop Dangerous Dolores Street 'Hill Bombing' Skateboard Events," https://www.cbsnews.com/sanfrancisco/news/officials-hope-speed-dots-will-stop-dangerous-dolores-street-hill-bombing-skateboard-events/.

Chiu, C., & Giamarino, C. (2019). "Creativity, Conviviality, and Civil Society in Neoliberalizing Public Space: Changing Politics and Discourses in Skateboarder Activism from New York City to Los Angeles." *Journal of Sport and Social Issues*, 43.6: 462–492.

City-Data.Com. (2021). "Mission Dolores neighborhood," https://www.city-data.com/neighborhood/Mission-Dolores-San-Francisco-CA.html.

Clark, S., & Sayers, E. (2023). "Skateparks as Communities of Care: The Role of Skateboarding in girls' and non-Binary youth's Mental Health Recovery During Lockdown." *Pedagogy, Culture & Society*, 2023: 1–20.

Coles, A. (2020). "Video Essay: A History of the VX1000." *Jenkem* 21 September 2020, https://www.jenkemmag.com/home/2020/09/21/history-vx1000-skatings-favorite-camera/.

Corwin, Z. B., Williams, N., Maruco, T., & Romero-Morales, M. (2019). *Beyond the Board: Skateboarding, Schools, and Society*. Los Angeles: Pullias Center for Higher Education.

Dean, N. (2023). *A Sociocultural Analysis of Adaptive Skateboarding and Wheelchair Motocross*. PhD Thesis: University of British Columbia.

Deb, A. (2023). *Wild Spaces in Urban Development: Grassroots Imaginaries in a Globalising World*. London: Taylor & Francis.

Dickinson, S., Millie, A., & Peters, E. (2022). "Street Skateboarding and the Aesthetic Order of Public Spaces." *The British Journal of Criminology*, 62.6: 1454–1469.

Evers, C. (2019). "Polluted Leisure." *Leisure Sciences*, 41.5: 423–440.

Evers, C. (2021). "Polluted Leisure and Blue Spaces: More-than-Human Concerns in Fukushima." *Journal of Sport and Social Issues*, 45.2: 179–195.

Gascon, M., Triguero-Mas, M., Martínez, D., Dadvand, P., Forns, J., Plasència, A., & Nieuwenhuijsen, M. J. (2015). "Mental Health Benefits of Long-Term Exposure to Residential Green and Blue Spaces: A Systematic Review." *International Journal of Environmental Research and Public Health*, 12.4: 4354–4379.

Geneshka, M., Coventry, P., Cruz, J., & Gilbody, S. (2021). "Relationship between Green and Blue Spaces with Mental and Physical Health: A Systematic Review of Longitudinal Observational Studies." *International Journal of Environmental Research and Public Health*, 18.17: 9010.

Glenney, B. (2024). "Skateboard Crime and the Pirating of Urban Spaces." *Crime, Media, and Culture*, 2024: 1–20.

Glenney, B., & O'Connor, P. (2019). "Skateparks as Hybrid Elements of the City." *Journal of Urban Design*, 24.6: 840–855.

Haraway, D. J. (2013). *When Species Meet*. Minneapolis: University of Minnesota Press.

Harmon, W., & Derrien, A. (2018). "Skateboarding, academia & public space: a conversation with Ocean Howell." *Free Skateboard Magazine*, https://www.freeskatemag.com/2018/08/15/skateboarding-academia-public-space-a-conversation-with-ocean-howell/.

Harrison-Caldwell, M. (2023) "Unlike Dolores Street, Skateboarding Won't Be a Crime at UN Plaza." *Medium*, 14 September 2023, https://thefrisc.com/unlike-dolores-street-skateboarding-wont-be-a-crime-at-un-plaza-f968a9cbba43.

Hölsgens, S. (2021). *Skateboarding in Seoul: A Sensory Ethnography*. Groningen: University of Groningen Press.

Hölsgens, S. (2024). "Learning to See or How to Make Sense of the Skillful Things Skateboarders Do." In Vannini, P. (ed.). *The Routledge International Handbook of Sensory Ethnography*, 387–400. New York: Routledge.

Holt, E. W., Lombard, Q. K., Best, N., Smiley-Smith, S., & Quinn, J. E. (2019). "Active and Passive Use of Green Space, Health, and Well-Being amongst University Students." *International Journal of Environmental Research and Public Health*, 16.3: Article 3.

Howell, O. (2001). "The Poetics of Security: Skateboarding, Urban Design, and the New Public Space." *Urban Action*, 2001: 64–86.

Howell, O. (2008). "Urban Governance, Recreation Space, and the Cultivation of Personal Responsibility." *Space and Culture*, 11.4: 475–496.

Jarosz, E. (2023). "Direct Exposure to Green and Blue Spaces Is Associated with Greater Mental Wellbeing in Older Adults." *Journal of Aging and Environment*, 37.4: 460–477.

Jonassen, W. & Holmes, S.W (2021). "The Rush and Risk of Skateboarding San Francisco's Hills." *The New Yorker*, https://www.newyorker.com/culture/video-dept/the-rush-and-risk-of-skateboarding-san-franciscos-hills.

Konvicka, M., Kuras, T., Liparova, J., Slezak, V., Horázná, D., Klečka, J., & Kleckova, I. (2021). "Low Winter Precipitation, but Not Warm Autumns and Springs, Threatens Mountain Butterflies in Middle-High Mountains." *PeerJ*, 9: e12021.

Langseth, T., & Salvesen, Ø. (2018). "Rock Climbing, Risk, and Recognition." *Frontiers in Psychology*, 9.1793: 1–10.

Lefebvre, H. (2014). *Toward an Architecture of Enjoyment*. Minneapolis: University of Minnesota Press.

Marr, L. C., & Ely, M. R. (2010). "Effect of Air Pollution on Marathon Running Performance." *Medicine and Science in Sports and Exercise*, 42.3: 585–591.

McDuie-Ra, D. (2022). "Skateboarding and the Mis-Use Value of Infrastructure." *ACME: An International Journal for Critical Geographies*, 21.1: 49–64.

Mitchao, D. P., Lewis, M., & Jakob, D., Benjamin, E. R., & Demetriades, D. (2022). "Skateboard Head Injuries: Are We Making Progress?" *Injury* 53.5: 1658–1661.

Myers, N. (2017). "Becoming Sensor in Sentient Worlds: A More-than-natural History of a Black Oak Savannah." In Bakke, G., & Peterson, M. (eds.). *Between Matter and Method: Encounters in Anthropology and Art*. London: Routledge.

O'Connor, P. (2019). *Skateboarding and Religion*. Springer Nature.

O'Connor, P., Evers, C., Glenney, B., & Willing, I. (2023). "Skateboarding in the Anthropocene: Grey Spaces of Polluted Leisure." *Leisure Studies* 42.6: 897–907.

Potter, J. D., Brooks, C., Donovan, G., Cunningham, C., & Douwes, J. (2023). "A Perspective on Green, Blue, and Grey Spaces, Biodiversity, Microbiota, and Human Health." *Science of The Total Environment*, 892, 164772. https://doi.org/10.1016/j.scitotenv.2023.164772.

Qvenild, M. (2014). "Wanted and Unwanted Nature: Landscape Development at Fornebu, Norway." *Journal of Environmental Policy & Planning*, 16.2: 183–200.

Radikonyana, P. S., Prinsloo, J. J., & Pelser, T. G. (2017). "The Contribution of Skateboarding to Societal Challenges." *African Journal of Hospitality, Tourism and Leisure*, 6.4: 2–20.

Romero, N. (2020). "You're Skating on Native Land: Queering and Decolonizing Skate Pedagogy." *Cultural and Pedagogical Inquiry*, 12.1: 230–243.

Rosenberger, R. (2018). "Why It Takes Both Postphenomenology and STS to Account for Technological Mediation." In Aagaard, J., Kyrre Berg Friis, J., Sorenson, J., Tafdrup, O., & Hasse, C. (eds.). *Postphenomenological Methodologies: New Ways in Mediating Techno-Human Relationships*, 171–198. Lanham: Rowman & Littlefield.

SFPD Commission. (2023) "Emails Regarding Delores Hill Bomb Event 2023." July 2023, https://www.sf.gov/sites/default/files/2023-07/Emails%20regarding%20Dolores%20Hill%20bomb%20event%203.pdf.

Simon, R. L., Torres, C. R., & Hager, P. F. (2015). *Fair Play: The Ethics of Sport*. Boulder: Westview Press.

Smith, O., & Raymen, T. (2018). "Deviant Leisure: A Criminological Perspective." *Theoretical Criminology*, 22.1: 63–82.

Stepansky, K., Delbert, T., & Bucey, J. C. (2023). "Therapeutic Impact of Engagement in Green Spaces." In Kuden, A., & Imrak, B. (eds.). *Urban Horticulture—Sustainable Gardening in Cities*, 85–104. London: IntechOpen.

Stoddart, M. C. (2011). ""If We Wanted to Be Environmentally Sustainable, We'd Take the Bus": Skiing, Mobility and the Irony of Climate Change." *Human Ecology Review*, 18.1: 19–29.

Tsing, A. T. (2015). *The Mushroom at the End of the World: On the Possibility of Life in Capitalist Ruins*. Princeton: Princeton University Press.

Turunen, A. W., Halonen, J., Korpela, K., Ojala, A., Pasanen, T., Siponen, T., Tiittanen, P., Tyrväinen, L., Yli-Tuomi, T., & Lanki, T. (2023). "Cross-sectional Associations of Different Types of Nature Exposure with Psychotropic, Antihypertensive and Asthma Medication. Occupational and Environmental Medicine." *Occupational and Environmental Medicine*, 80.2: 111–118.

Vivoni, F. (2009). "Spots of Spatial Desire: Skateparks, Skateplazas, and Urban Politics." *Journal of Sport and Social Issues*, 33.2: 130–149.

Wergeland, E. S., & Hognestad, H. K. (2021). "Reusing Stadiums for a Greener Future: the Circular Design Potential of Football Architecture." *Frontiers in Sports and Active Living* 3.692632.

Willing, I., Bennett, A., Thorpe, H., & Green, B. (2023). "Ageing in DIY and Alternative Cultures: Exploring Forms of Masculinity and Adult Play in Jackass Forever." *DIY, Alternative Cultures & Society*, 2.1: 1–14.

Willing, I., & Pappalardo, A. (2023). *Skateboarding, Power and Change*. Berlin: Springer.

Zajchowski, C. A., & Rose, J. (2020). "Sensitive Leisure: Writing the Lived Experience of Air Pollution." *Leisure Sciences*, 42.1: 1–14.

6 Epilogue
Toward a Multispecies Futurity for Skateboarding

As soon as you try to define skateboarding, it becomes something else. Skate video *Sonagi* captures this sensation by claiming that skateboarding can be "quick and impactful like a sudden rain shower" (Kim 2019). Two minutes into the video, we see rain wetting the hardpan city surfaces, reflecting its grey-brown modernist architecture. What follows are close-ups of the street: an alleyway, some industrial tools, and standing water. We turn to an undercroft, given prominence by its graffitied plastered walls. Entering the frame is Daegeun Ahn, one of Korea's most elegant skaters. Known for his rapid succession of technical tricks, Ahn spends much of his spare time scouting for unusual spots matching his imaginative, enskiled aptitude. As the editor of the *Draobetaks* zine (2011–2015) and contributor to YouTube channel *Daily Grind*, he documents Seoul's urban renewal projects – taking photographs of spots that risk destruction.

In *Sonagi*, Ahn is perfecting his city craft. The video's opening sequence exposes his ability to scan any urban space for its skateability. In between two pillars, he performs a bs bluntslide, a sensorially awkward and exceptionally technical trick. What's commonplace – the concrete foundation and asphalted road underneath a bridge – is turned into a site for creativity, performance, and expression. "To us," Ben Goldfarb (2023: 9–10) writes, "roads are so mundane they're practically invisible; to wildlife, they're utterly alien. Other species perceive the world through senses we cannot fathom and experience stressors and enticements we hardly register." To Ahn, mundane architecture is neither alien nor mundane: as an avid skater, he recognizes diverse shapes and surfaces amidst a homogeneous-built environment. Such skills come at a cost: later in the video, we as spectators see how Ahn breaks his arm, revealing the danger of modern architecture. Hostility emerges as soon as you divert from a city's intended use-case. The city of Seoul is no exception.

One of the city's functional obstacles is a knee-height cement quarter pipe ramp, inventively walling the pavement from grasses and weeds. The ramp's purpose is somewhat unclear, not least because it escapes its expected role as accessible design: it is too steep for most wheeled activities, while it leads nowhere but a field of wild growth. Despite the ramp's sober concrete aesthetics,

DOI: 10.4324/9781003510642-6
This chapter has been made available under a CC-BY-NC-ND 4.0 license.

Ahn sees an opportunity for trick play. Sliding across its edge, Ahn positions himself between the smooth greyness of the ramp and the untidy greens of wild growth. Touching the grasses with the edge of his board, he briefly shares a microhabitat with urban greens – and their sway of spontaneity and nonconformity (Deb 2023). Ahn's reappropriation of the city manifests a skillset of finding salubrious pleasure among hostile architecture, drawing attention to a surprisingly diverse ecology. As a city craft, skateboarding generates an opportunity for practitioners to, as Zajchowski and Rose (2020: 11) write, "take control of their stories": theirs can be one of environmentalism, of negotiating a multispecies urbanity, of making the city somewhat of a friendlier place, and of injecting an artistic grammar into hackneyed spaces.

A sensory futurity

More than half of the world's population is urban, and almost a third will live in cities by 2070 (Kadakia and Galea 2023). Humanity is slowly becoming an urban animal. And yet, our cities are in crisis: our health systems are in disrepair, food deserts proliferate, infectious diseases multiply, and inter-urban inequities accelerate. The livability of cities is thus under threat, resulting in untenable conditions rarely seen in human history. For sociologist Des Fitzgerald (2023), this precarity coincides with an urban anxiety: entire demographics are helplessly waiting for a utopian fantasy, one that today appears naively cloaked in organic greens. What urbanites are missing is not just secure housing, nutritious food, political and personal autonomy, and spaces of play and leisure: they also need forest baths and wild swims.

So, is there any salubrity to be gained by living in cities? Skaters may say: to play is to attend to one's health and wellbeing. To feel the texture of bricks or polished granite throughout your entire body, to read the city through foot feel and its sonic swaying, is a matter of sensory attunement. To roll through a city and to see, hear, feel, and even smell its play potentialities make you feel alive. Skateboarding, to paraphrase Fitzgerald (2023: 12), is like a glitch, "something unexpectedly grey and graceful, something clean and sharp and new, [to] cut through the landscape." To craft the city for trick play is to realize its potential for health, creativity, and wellness, as much as it foregrounds the inescapable toxicity of urban life. Neither naively hopeful nor desperately cynical, the act of moving sideways affords a grounded positionality: to skate is to directly engage the city – sensorially, socially, and ecologically.

What are we to make of the skater's way of sensing the city, their sensorial attunement, and emplaced zones of interest that approach religious zeal and ritual? Many skaters fail to articulate or even acknowledge their bodily techniques as pieces of knowledge. Adept observers, like the French public intellectual David Abiker (2022), have described skaters as "philosophes du bitumen" (philosophers of the streets) and "un *Mystère* sure roues" (a mystery on wheels). It is their very locale which generates Abiker's praise, "'Let's make them skatepark' sing the neighbors. Fools! That will totally extinguish the charm of skateboarding, for all that is attractive about skating is taking hold of a territory that was not made for it."[1] But if skaters are street philosophers, how then is their knowledge acquired? Where are their theses? Who bestows their publications, degrees, and pedigree? How does a skateable space pose an area of philosophical inquiry: a problem?

The stoics had their porch, Socrates his square, Angela Davis her square and enforced prison cell, Sophie Oluwole her classroom, and the skaters their city spots. They profess through acts of spectacle and educate through their silent coolness. "They do not know the knowledge that only they possess,"[2] shouts Abiker. But perhaps they do know. Through enskilment, skaters learn to train their senses to navigate their socio-spatial surroundings: they find skateable space, challenge the dominant order of the city, make their own interventions, and build grassroots communities. Tarmac and polished granite are the basis of a horizontal and crafts-like pedagogy of the city, a path tracing how it feels to become enworlded as a skater in relation to others. Individual or collective, emancipatory or competitive, masculine or queer: skateboarding is a spectrum one navigates by moving and performing across time and space. It is learned by doing, not least by navigating one's role as both friend and foe to the city.

Our sensory anthropology of skateboarding reflects how a skater's stance is located on the axes of gender, ethnicity, age, geography, class, and mobility. In so doing, we acknowledge that the phenomenal experience of riding a board or identifying skateable space may not only feel different to all practitioners but also hold situated and potentially contradictory meanings. As such, we propose a break from the singular ontology of skateboarding and instead suggest a commitment to *skateboardings* (Callan-Riley and Hölsgens 2020). Throughout the book, we zoom in on the somatic heritage of individual skaters to zoom out on the societies that construct normative forms of embodiment and enskilment (cf. Abulhawa 2020; Hölsgens 2024). The sensory density of skateboarding benefits from an anthropological lens, which encourages us to elaborate on how a skater's sensory model is socially constructed, historically conditioned, and culturally informed.

Our book is not an exhaustive study of all possible models of skate. Rather, we use our insider's perspective as skaters-turned-researchers to articulate a lens, methodology, and sensibility for fellow researchers to take up, alter, and make their own. Our case studies speak to issues we deem most pressing in skateboarding today: the commodification of leisure activities, neoliberal and meritocratic narratives of success and failure, the privatization of public space, the pollution of our cities, and inequality of opportunity. If skateboarding becomes just another sport, another commodity to sell goods or win medals, or another pastime to look back on with nostalgic purchases, it is a dead craft. We hope that skaters continue to refract their future through inimitable dispersion, increased plurality, growing solidarity, and ecological concern. Only then will they – *will we* – effect social change through our shared city craft.

Notes

1 "leur des pistes! > couinera le riverain. Surtout pas, ça casserait le charme; car tout l'attrait du skate, e'est d'occuper un terrain pas fait pour ça."
2 "de sagesse qu'ils ne soupçonnent pas eux-memes."

References

Abiker, D. (2022) *Le skate, ça fait u bruit. Je me dis cela en passant par les escaliers*, https://www.instagram.com/p/CZ1ZeXar7n7/?igshid=MTc4MmM1YmI2Ng%3D%3D, accessed 29 April 2024.

Abulhawa, D. (2020). *Skateboarding and Femininity: Gender, Space-Making and Expressive Movement*. London: Routledge.

Callan-Riley, T., & Hölsgens, S. (2020). *Urban Pamphleteer# 8 Skateboardings*. London: Urban Laboratory.

Deb, A. (2023). *Wild Spaces in Urban Development: Grassroots Imaginaries in a Globalising World*. London: Taylor & Francis.

Fitzgerald, D. (2023). *The Living City: Why Cities Don't Need to Be Green to Be Great*. United States: Basic Books.

Goldfarb, B. (2023). *Crossings: How Road Ecology Is Shaping the Future of Our Planet*. New York: W.W. Norton.

Hölsgens, S. (2024). "Learning to See or How to Make Sense of the Skillful Things Skateboarders Do." In Vannini, P. (ed.). *The Routledge International Handbook of Sensory Ethnography*, 387–400. New York: Routledge.

Kadakia, K. T., & Galea, S. (2023). "Urbanization and the Future of Population Health." *The Milbank Quarterly*, 101: 153–175.

Kim, J. Y. (2019). *Sonagi*, 17 min, https://www.youtube.com/watch?v=Y1y0CQwqaT0, last accessed 20 March 2024.

Zajchowski, C. A., & Rose, J. (2020). "Sensitive Leisure: Writing the Lived Experience of Air Pollution." *Leisure Sciences*, 42.1: 1–14.

Index

Abiker, David 78–79
Abulhawa, Dani 24–25, 38, 40–41, 60
adaptive skateboarding 63, 65
aesthetic 18–19, 33–36, 50, 60, 68–69; order 36, 40, 47, 62, 67, 69
Ahmed, Sara 7, 19–20
Ahn, Daegeun 77–78
anthropology 6, 32; method 5–7, 79; practice 6, 8, 10, 14, 25; of the senses 1, 9, 10, 25, 79
architecture 1, 21, 38, 43, 69, 77; hostile 4, 37; landscape 34, 64, 72; sacred 5; skate spots 24, 30, 36, 40, 43, 72, 78

Bäckström, Åsa 25
Ballard, Taylor 8, 17, 23
Barrow Ted 2–4
battle 47, 52; handrail 32–33
Beachy, Kyle 46, 60
Beal, Becky 4, 24, 33, 51, 55
Berrics, The 52
blindness 63
Blubba, The 35–36, 40
blue space 63
body 51; aging 46; damage 51, 68; digital 36; gendered 24; knowledge 5, 10, 16, 40, 51; practices 10, 21, 48–49, 54, 63–64; racial 20; schema 17; sensing 30, 78; skill 22, 40; stance 13–14, 18, 23; study of 6, 9, 15, 19; sympathy 36, 47; tool 16, 32
Borden, Iain 4, 21–22, 37
Brownfields 39, 62
Bryggeriet 56
Burnside 71

Callan-Riley, Thom 10, 36, 79
care 2, 3, 11, 42, 52, 57, 64; community 7, 8, 52, 55; spot 39, 42, 60

Chamarette, Jenny 5, 30
Civid, Leeds 42–43
Classen, Constance 9
colonialism 38
community 30, 42–43, 46, 53–56, 64–65, 67; academic 4–5, 8; craft 16, 32, 42; gendered 25, 53–56; skate 7, 33, 38, 40–41, 67
Coughlin-Bogue, Tobias 41
craft 16, 32, 70; body 31–32; city 10–11, 30, 32, 35–37, 40, 43, 69, 72, 77–79; grey craft 64, 69; sensory 16, 39, 78; *see also* enskilment; skill
creativity 1, 3, 7, 70, 73, 78; assemblage 33, 60; media 33–36; skill 21, 40; tricks 21, 33–35, 40, 77
culture, skate 1, 4, 6–7, 9, 20, 38, 55, 58; craft 10–11, 14, 16; spiritual 50, 53, 64; sport 34; subculture 1, 18, 41; urban 4, 25, 46, 61, 67
curb 2–3, 5, 21, 31, 34–35, 39–41, 64, 72

D'Amico-Samuels, Deborah 7
Dahlquist, John 56
Deleuze, Gilles 36–37
Delfino, Fabiana 8
desire, spots of 37–39, 72; path 31
DIY 9; craft 32; parks 5; spots 39, 42
Dolores Street, hill bomb 66–70
dysbiosis 62, 70

Ebeling, Kristen 24, 33, 51, 54–55
ecology 61, 72; of culture 46; of practice 5; sensory 5, 6; urban 39, 64, 78
ecosophy 36–37
El Toro 24–25
EMB (Embarcadero) 34
embodiment 9, 19, 33, 36, 79

Index

enskilment 1, 6, 10, 16, 20, 23–24, 30, 36, 48, 64, 72, 79; defined 2; *see also* skill
environment 15, 40, 51, 55, 60, 63, 73; assemblage 16, 21, 24; built 1–3, 10–11, 14, 16, 22, 29–31, 36, 39–40, 51, 53, 67, 72–73, 77; pollution 9, 61–62, 69
epistemology 9–11, 22, 29, 37; gnarly 51; heel 33–35; know-how 16, 34–35; sonic 5, 31; *see also* knowledge
equilibrioception 23, 26
ethnography 3, 5, 9; rolling 6
Evers, Clifton 1, 61–62, 73
expertise 6, 16, 32, 37, 48; expert 32, 37, 48

Farrar, Una 30
femininity 6, 9, 19, 24
fetishism 1, 37, 39; spots 53, 62
film 2, 7, 18, 29–30, 54, 56; filmer 7, 18, 26, 33–34, 38, 47, 50
Fitzgerald, Des 78
Fujisawa, Nanaka 32–33

gaze 18, 20, 23–25, 31; male 24–25; skater's eye 21–24, 25, 29, 53
Geckle, Bethany 9, 56–57
gender 4, 10, 21, 24–26, 32, 38, 40–41, 63, 79
gliding 16
Goldfarb, Ben 77
Grasseni, Cristina 9
green space 31, 34, 61–68, 71–73, 78
grey space 3, 10–11, 39, 47, 61–64, 67–69, 72; craft 64, 69
grym 25
Guattari, Félix 36–37

Halprin, Lawrence 33–34
Haraway, Donna 21–23, 73
Harris, Anna 9, 20, 51
Health 2, 25, 41, 52, 60–63, 66, 72, 78
Heidegger, Martin 15, 17
Howell, Ocean 4, 70–71
Howes, David 9, 25, 53
Hsu, Jerry 18–20, 24
Huston, Nyjah 9, 24–25

Ibarra, Norma 55
Ingold, Tim 16, 31–32
instruction 10; coaches 10, 25, 48; *see also* pedagogy

Jacobs, Candy 24, 38
Jones, Tyshawn 37

Kadow, Ben 35–36
kinesthesia 14; balance 18, 23
Kirchart, Heath 47–48, 52–53
knowledge 5, 10, 22, 35–38, 41, 48, 61, 64, 68, 79; bodily 33, 51, 78; tacit 24, 48, 61, 73; *see also* epistemology

Latour, Bruno 34
Leal, Rayssa 50
ledge 2, 31, 34–35, 39, 42–43, 64, 72
Lefebvre, Henri 69
leisure 1, 6, 13, 61–62, 64, 67, 69, 78–79; deviant 65–67; polluted 1, 61–62, 69; sensitive 73; vs. sport 1, 6
lifeworld 3, 7
Lilley, Ruby 23
Long, Helena 30, 55
LOVE Park 43
Low, Kevin 52

Malmö 2, 30, 43, 56, 60
Marks, Laura 29, 36
masculinity 33, 40
materiality 3, 29
Mauss, Marcel 9
McDuie-Ra, Duncan 5, 37, 39, 42, 64, 67; rolling ethnography 6
Meadley, Harry 42
media 5, 24, 32, 46, 54; social 19, 30
Menke, Louisa 39, 49
Merleau-Ponty, Maurice 15, 17–18
methodology 5–7, 30, 64, 79; ethnographic 6; rolling 6
Meurle, Sarah 2
Miner, Jon 18–20
Misophonia 26
modernism 34, 43
mushrooms 10, 64

narrative 7, 20, 43, 70; failure 11, 47, 51–53, 56–57, 79; masculine 24, 38, 55
neurodiversity 26
NIMBY 67
noticing 10, 32, 36
Nowodworski, Pao 23
Nunes, Felipe 41

O'Connor, Paul 1, 6, 37, 39, 43, 46, 50, 60–61, 69
ocularcentrism 14, 22, 24
Olympics 9–10, 51–52, 62

Pálsson, Gísli 16
Pappalardo, Anthony (skater) 35–36, 40
Pappalardo, Anthony (writer) 5, 6, 20, 54, 61
pedagogy 60; enskilment 10; failure 50, 57; horizontal 9, 79; noticing 32
perception 6, 15, 20, 24; bodily 10, 23, 25
performance 4, 8, 20, 32, 35, 37, 40, 48, 57; aesthetic 6, 24, 68, 77; athletic 25–26, 31, 50–51, 60; divergent 21, 26, 57
phenomenology 6, 15, 19, 48, 55
photography 32–33, 38, 77
place 3, 16–17, 29, 37, 42, 66, 78; emplacement 9, 11, 14, 16, 22, 24, 30, 33, 36, 78; nonplace 33, 40; place-making 21, 26, 32
play 1, 7, 13, 21–22, 30, 32–33, 36, 40, 47–51, 73, 78; deviant 26, 72; playground 67; writing 8
pleasure 5, 18, 20, 39, 50–53, 55, 67, 69, 78; grey 11, 60–61, 68–70; risk 48, 67–69
poetics 2, 4, 20, 32, 51
political 1, 7, 10, 14–15, 18–19, 25, 57, 78; prefigurative 54, 68–69
pollution 1–2, 9, 23, 69, 79; social 69–70
positionality 4–6, 9–10, 14, 21, 26, 37, 47, 55, 61, 69–70, 78
practice 1–2, 54–55; care 11, 13, 64; communities of 10, 18, 25, 42, 38, 63–64; skilled 6, 10, 14, 16, 26, 48–49
proprioception 14, 18, 26
Pushing Boarders 3–5, 24, 38, 56–57

queer 19, 41, 79
queering 7, 11; failure 54–56; phenomenology 19–20

Redondo, Don 21–24; *see also* seeing, skater's eye
resistance 1, 9, 25, 72
rhizome 37
risk 11, 23–24, 48, 52, 55, 66–70
ritual 1, 5, 48–51, 57, 78

salubrious 61–64, 72, 79
scene 5, 38
Sedo, Tim 37
seeing 14, 18, 24–25, 33; skater's eye 21–22; practices of 64; *see also* vision; visual

senses 5, 9, 14, 30, 77, 79; mediation 10, 21, 25, 33, 36; multi-sense 6, 29, 73
sensorium 19–20
sidewalk 26, 31, 34; surfers 13, 41
skateboard 5, 17, 47, 50, 60, 63, 66, 68; body 46, 63; craft 10, 37, 43; tool 4, 16, 26, 31, 34, 38, 40, 51, 60, 70
skateboardings 10, 40, 46, 56–57, 79; *Skateboardings* 2, 40
Skate Like A Girl (SLAG) 46, 53–56
skate spots 30, 34–8, 39–43, 46, 52–53; *see also* grey space
skill 32, 46; acquisition 24, 48–50; hard/ soft skill 32, 57; *see also* enskilment
Sisyphus 50
site 5, 10, 14, 22, 29–30, 34, 37–38, 77
Slow Impact 20
Soto, Felix 34–35
somatic 1, 5–6, 17–9, 52, 64, 79
Sonagi (film) 77
sound 5, 13, 22, 29–30, 34
sport 1, 9–10, 32, 61, 63, 79
stance 13–15, 17–21, 24–26, 50, 51, 68, 73; social 25–26, 69, 79; switch 18–21, 57
Stay Gold (film) 18–20
Steamer, Elissa 57
street 31, 34, 41, 72, 77; architecture 1, 22, 32, 61; culture 25; philosopher 79; skating 1, 52; trees 64
Street League 50–51
subversion 17–18, 31, 35, 65, 68–69
Superfund site 62
surface 3, 16, 21–22, 26, 30–33, 36, 40, 47, 51, 61, 68, 77
surfing 13–14, 19, 62

tacit knowledge 4, 9, 16, 24, 26, 48, 51, 61, 68, 73
taskspace 16
Tassopoulos, Johnny 17
techniques 7, 9–10, 15, 17–20, 23, 31–33, 48, 53, 68, 78; bodily 2, 14, 24–25, 35–36
texturology 22
This is Skateboarding (film) 46–47, 52, 54
Thrasher (magazine) 2, 21, 24, 37, 46, 53
Timpson, Zane 66, 68
Tomczyk, Perry 65
tradition 40, 60; non- 41, 56, 67
Transenders (film) 54–57

travel 37, 39, 41, 48, 53; writing 13, 38
Tsing, Anna 10, 64

Unity (skate collective) 41
Universal Design 41
urban planning 31, 69

video *see* film; photography
vision *see* seeing

Vivoni, Francis 21, 42, 72
VX1000 47, 60

WCMX 63
White, Shari 30
Willing, Indigo 5, 6, 20, 54, 61, 66

zine 2, 77

For Product Safety Concerns and Information please contact our EU representative GPSR@taylorandfrancis.com
Taylor & Francis Verlag GmbH, Kaufingerstraße 24, 80331 München, Germany